The Battle
of Glorieta Pass

The Battle of Glorieta Pass

*A Gettysburg
in the West,
March 26–28, 1862*

Thomas S. Edrington
and John Taylor

University of New Mexico Press
Albuquerque

© 1998 by the University of New Mexico Press
Printed in the United States of America

19   18   17   16   15   5   6   7   8   9

ISBN-13: 978-0-8263-2287-6
ISBN-13: 0-8263-2287-5

Library of Congress-in-Publication Data

Edrington, Thomas S., 1936–
The battle of Glorieta Pass: a Gettysburg in the West, March 26–28, 1862 /
Thomas S. Edrington and John Taylor.
—1st ed.
        p.   cm.
Includes bibliographical references and index.
ISBN 0-8263-1896-7 (cloth)
ISBN 0-8263-2287-5 (pbk.)
1. Glorieta Pass (N.M.), Battle of, 1862.
I. Taylor, John, 1947–   .
II. Title.
E473.4.E37
973.7'31—dc21
97-44498
CIP

Contents

Illustrations VI

Maps VIII

Acknowledgments IX

1. War in New Mexico 3

2. Bloody Valverde 13

3. Marches—North and South 23

4. Encounter in Apache Canyon 41

5. Interlude 57

6. Collision at Pigeon's Ranch 63

7. Confederate Victory 77

8. Disaster at Johnson's Ranch 89

9. Aftermath 101

10. Reprise 113

Appendix: Union and Confederate Order of Battle, Unit Strengths, and Casualties 123

Notes 143

Bibliography 161

Index 169

List of Illustrations

Pigeon's Ranch in 1880   *frontispiece*
Lieutenant Colonel John Baylor, Second Texas Mounted Volunteers   8
Major Isaac Lynde, USA   8
Brigadier General Henry Hopkins Sibley, CSA   10
Colonel Edward Canby, Nineteenth U.S. Infantry   16
Fort Union in 1856   18
The Fort Union "Star Fort" in 1862   18
Plan of Fort Union   19
Colonel Tom Green, Fifth Texas Mounted Volunteers   20
Lieutenant Colonel Benjamin Roberts, Fifth New Mexico
     Volunteers   20
The Final Charge on McRae's Battery   22
Captain Herbert Enos, U.S. Quartermaster Corps   26
William "Old Bill" Davidson, Fifth Texas Mounted Volunteers   27
Colorado Territorial Governor William Gilpin   29
Major Charles Pyron, Second Texas Mounted Volunteers   35
Major John "Shrop" Shropshire, Fifth Texas Mounted Volunteers   35
Colonel Gabriel Paul, Fourth New Mexico Volunteers   37
Colonel John Slough, First Colorado Volunteers   37

Major John Chivington, First Colorado Volunteers   39
Captain Edward Wynkoop, First Colorado Volunteers   45
Captain Scott Anthony, First Colorado Volunteers   45
Captain Jacob Downing, First Colorado Volunteers   49
Pyron's Bastion   53
Painting of the Strategic Bridge in Apache Canyon   54
Colonel William Scurry, Fourth Texas Mounted Volunteers   59
Pigeon's Ranch in 1880   65
Lieutenant Colonel Samuel Tappan, First Colorado Volunteers   67
Major Henry Raguet, Fourth Texas Mounted Volunteers   69
Some Officers of the Colorado Volunteers   71
Captain Denman Shannon, Fifth Texas Mounted Volunteers   82
Captain Samuel Logan, First Colorado Volunteers   91
Painting of the Union Raid on Johnson's Ranch   96
Lieutenant Colonel Manuel Chaves, Second New Mexico Volunteers   99
Alexander Grzelachowski   100
Reburial of the Confederate dead at the Santa Fe National Cemetery   121

List of Maps

1. The Southwest in 1862 2
2. The Confederate Invasion Route 2
3. Glorieta Pass 2
4. The Route of the Coloradans to Glorieta Pass 32
5. Confederate Advance Toward Fort Union 33
6. The Skirmish at Apache Canyon—first phase 46
7. The Skirmish at Apache Canyon—second phase 48
8. The Skirmish at Apache Canyon—third phase 52
9. The Battle of Pigeon's Ranch—first phase 74
10. The Battle of Pigeon's Ranch—early second phase 79
11. The Battle of Pigeon's Ranch—late second phase 81
12. The Battle of Pigeon's Ranch—third phase 85
13. Chivington's Route to and from Johnson's Ranch 93
14. Glorieta Today 119

Acknowledgments

THE AUTHORS WOULD LIKE TO RECOGNIZE THE CONTRIBUTION AND assistance provided by the staffs at the U. S. National Archives, the Texas State Library, the Museum of New Mexico, the Harold B. Simpson Confederate Research Center at Hill College, the New Mexico Highlands University Library, the University of Texas Center for American History, the Special Collections Branch of the Zimmerman Library at the University of New Mexico, and the Special Collections Branch of the Albuquerque Public Library. In addition, we owe a special debt of gratitude to Garry Brown, Steve Dupree, Wes and Judy Bowyer Martin, and Rich Preston for their thorough and insightful reviews of the manuscript; and to David Cunnington for his superb computer graphic support. We would also like to acknowledge the consistent encouragement and support for this project provided by David Holtby and the staff at the University of New Mexico Press. Finally, we note that without the enthusiasm and support of our wives, Daphne and Lynn, this labor of love would never have come to fruition.

TOM EDRINGTON AND JOHN TAYLOR

The Battle
of Glorieta Pass

The Confederate Invasion Route

The Southwest in 1862

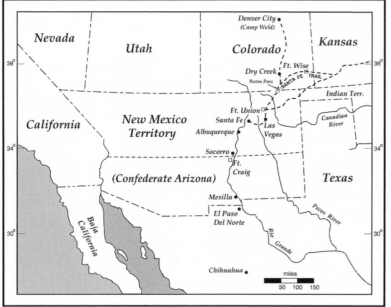

Glorieta Pass

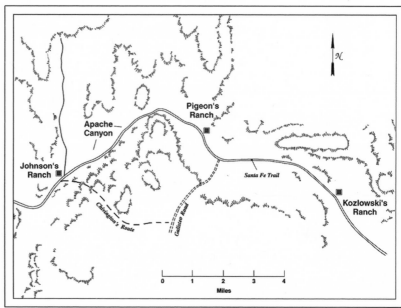

(Graphics by David Cunnington)

1

War in New Mexico

THE NEWLY PROMOTED CONFEDERATE COLONEL SAT ASTRIDE HIS horse on the Santa Fe Trail and looked east from beneath the brim of a dirty, sweat-stained hat, savoring the glow of satisfaction as the smells, sounds, and adrenaline of battle faded away. For the second time in just over a month, the view in his binoculars consisted of the backs of blue uniforms in full retreat. His Texans had done it again. Another battlefield was theirs!

Yet some details troubled the forty-one-year-old lawyer from San Augustine, Texas. First, the battlefield had not been won without cost. He would not know for sure how many men he had lost for several hours; but now that the roar of the cannons and the whine of the minié balls had subsided, he could hear the moans and cries of the wounded echoing through the canyon. He knew that his officer corps had suffered the loss of two majors and at least one captain, and he could only guess that others had been wounded. In fact the sting of the wound on his own cheek and the bullet holes in his trousers brought the reality of battle all too close to home.

And then there were the rumors of a major Federal force several miles behind the Confederate lines. It was said that men had galloped in from the base camp at the mouth of the canyon telling of an attack on his supply train. Surely this was not true. After all, his own force occupied the only road back to the camp. But where was that giant of a Union major who had given the boys such a bad time two days before, the one the Union prisoners called the "Fighting Parson?" No one had seen him anywhere during the day, yet he was clearly one of the Union commander's trusted aides.

These speculations quickly yielded to reality, however. The Texans were both victorious and exhausted and their colonel had to consolidate his position—there was work to do and daylight was fading fast.

The day was March 28, 1862, and the American Civil War was in full swing. In Virginia, George McClellan's Army of the Potomac was moving "on to Richmond" in the early stages of the Peninsula Campaign. At Kernstown, Stonewall Jackson had just suffered the only loss of his storied Shenandoah Valley Campaign. The *Monitor* and the *Merrimac* had just made naval history with their classic duel in Hampton Roads. And in Tennessee, Forts Henry and Donelson had fallen to federal forces under Ulysses S. Grant. It is no wonder then that the fractured and excited nation took scant notice of a confrontation in the far-off Territory of New Mexico, where a small force of Texans was wrestling with a federal command, mostly Coloradans, in a narrow defile about twenty-five miles east of Santa Fe.

The day would come, however, when the Battle of Glorieta Pass would begin to take on a measure of importance, and several writers would go so far as to call Glorieta the "Gettysburg of the West." No one knows for sure who coined the phrase, but it is not surprising that someone would make the analogy.[1] Both engagements resulted from a Confederate invasion of Union territory; both were three-day affairs; and both could be called high-water marks of the respective Confederate campaigns. Even so, as the details of the story unfold, it will become clear that the analogy between Glorieta and Gettysburg is far from a perfect one and perhaps serves the novelist better than it does the historian.

The coming of the Civil War to New Mexico was probably inevitable. The Southern Confederacy, no less than the Old Union, figured it had a Manifest Destiny to reach the Pacific Coast, and control of the Territory of New Mexico was obviously a very large and direct step toward that goal. In addition the inextricably linked issues of slavery in the territories and the continued push for statehood had been part of New Mexico politics and the national agenda for more than a decade. In the aftermath of the war with Mexico, there was a clear antislavery sentiment in the territory; however the appointment of a number of southerners to the territorial governorship caused attitudes to shift. By 1859 the territorial legislature had adopted a slave code that was signed by Governor Abraham Rencher on February 3 of that year.

Nonetheless, most New Mexicans cared not at all about North–South politics and simply harbored the hope that somehow they would be spared the ravages of war. Their feelings were well represented by the editor of the *Santa Fe Gazette*:

> What is the position of New Mexico? The answer is a short one. She desires to be let alone. No interferences from one side or the other of the sections that are now waging war. She neither wants abolitionists nor secessionists from abroad to mix in her affairs at present; nor will she tolerate either. In her own good time, she will say her say, and choose for herself the position she wishes to occupy in the new disposition of the now disrupted power of the United States.[2]

The sentiment of the people as echoed by the newspaperman was clearly wishful thinking, as most New Mexicans probably realized. In fact many of New Mexico's Hispanics feared, or even expected, that one day the Texans would return and exact vengeance for the treachery and cruel treatment inflicted upon the members of the Texan–Santa Fe Expedition by New Mexico's governor Manuel Armijo in 1841. It is said that some New Mexican mothers would admonish their children by telling them, "If you are not good, I'll give you to the Tejanos, who are coming back."[3]

On the other hand, the Anglos of the southern communities, who had for some time sought to separate themselves from the "alien" population of Santa Fe and the north, were hoping the Texans *would* come. After the U.S. Congress had rejected some ten bills seeking to carve a new territory out of the southern part of New Mexico, the citizens took matters into their own hands. Delegates to a convention at Tucson in early April 1860 proclaimed that all of New Mexico south of 33°40' was henceforth the Territory of Arizona. Four counties were established, a provisional constitution was drafted, and Dr. Lewis S. Owings, formerly a Texas legislator, was elected territorial governor.[4]

Although the U.S. Congress declined to recognize the proceedings of the convention, there would soon be another option available for the creation of an Arizona Territory. When Texas joined the roll of seceding states, the politicians in southern New Mexico lost little time in casting their lot with the Confederacy. Two separate conventions held in March 1861—one in Mesilla and one in Tucson—passed resolutions to repudiate the Union and join the Confederate States of America.[5]

Texans were delighted with the course of events in New Mexico, but they realized that the 1,500 U.S. troops stationed in the territory on their western border still presented a problem. Whereas the federal forces in Texas evacuated peacefully—with some encouragement from the Texas militia—no such move was made in New Mexico. On the contrary, units were called in from the western forts (Buchanan, Breckenridge, Fauntleroy, and McLane) to posts on or east of the Rio Grande, where their attention would be directed less to the hostile Indians and more toward the new adversaries from Texas and the Confederacy.[6]

When authorities in Texas ousted the U.S. Army, they insisted that all Federal troops leave by way of the coast. This measure precluded a military buildup in New Mexico and also assured that military stores would not be removed from their "rightful" location. Fort Bliss, near El Paso in far West Texas, presented a special problem. Even though the Federal commander there, Lieutenant Colonel I. V. D. Reeve, complied with the rules set down by the Texans, that particular post with six pieces of artillery and other valuable supplies was much more accessible to the Federal command at Fort Fillmore (only forty miles to the north) than it was to the Texan forces four hundred miles away at San Antonio.[7]

The task of securing the abandoned posts in the more remote parts of South and West Texas was assigned to the ten companies of the Second Regiment, Texas Mounted Volunteers, which had been mustered into Confederate service on May 23, 1861. Colonel John S. Ford took four companies of the regiment to the lower Rio Grande, while Lieutenant Colonel John R. Baylor headed west with the other six to garrison Forts Lancaster, Davis, Stockton, Clark, and Bliss. When Baylor arrived at Fort Bliss in mid July, all government property seemed to be in place.[8]

Born in Bourbon County, Kentucky, thirty-four-year-old John Baylor migrated west, settled on a ranch near Weatherford, and became the quintessential Texan. He stood six-foot-three, weighed 230 pounds, had a natural inclination toward combat, and displayed the lone star emblem on a large belt buckle made from the silver hair ornament worn by a Comanche he had killed on the Brazos in 1858.[9] After moving to Texas in 1840, he promptly began a career as an Indian fighter, state legislator, and Indian agent. A devout secessionist, he wrote in 1856, "I hope to heaven we have a war . . . the sooner the better." In December 1860, two months before the referendum on secession, Baylor began to recruit the troops he would lead into New Mexico.[10]

Despite the absence of Federal initiative, Lieutenant Colonel Baylor assumed that the U.S. forces concentrating at Fort Fillmore intended to attack his command at Fort Bliss. Preferring to be on the offensive, the aggressive lieutenant colonel moved into New Mexico with 258 men and occupied the town of Mesilla on July 25, 1861.[11]

Fort Fillmore was under the command of Major Isaac Lynde, Seventh U.S. Infantry, a native of Vermont with thirty-four years of service in the U.S. Army. According to James McKee, assistant surgeon at the post, Lynde's gray hair and beard gave him a venerable appearance that complemented his reticent manner, "giving the impression of wisdom and knowledge of his profession . . . [an officer who] could be depended on to defend the honor of the flag."[12]

Major Lynde brought four companies of the Seventh Infantry from Fort McLane to Fort Fillmore in early July. By the time of Baylor's arrival at Mesilla, the garrison at Fillmore comprised seven companies of the Seventh and three of Mounted Rifles, some five hundred men all together. With this force, the major had declared that he had "very little fear of the result of any attack . . . from Texas."[13]

Even so, Major Lynde realized that Fort Fillmore, lying in a basin surrounded by chaparral-covered sand hills, was not particularly well suited for defense. Probably for that reason he decided to take the fight beyond the confines of the fort. On the afternoon of July 25 he marched his force out of Fort Fillmore and attacked Baylor in Mesilla. It was a brief affair, however, as the stout defense put up by the Texans soon took the nerve out of the Federal commander and he elected to call it quits and return to the fort.

Now fearing that he could not hold the fort against this surprisingly capable adversary, Lynde decided to move his command to Fort Stanton, 150 miles to the northeast. Though heavily outnumbered, Baylor pursued the Federals as they fled toward San Augustin Pass; and when he overtook Lynde's strung-out column, the faint-hearted Union major simply surrendered his command in what one of his subalterns called the "most humiliating and disgraceful event that has ever blurred . . . the splendid record of the Regular Army."[14]

By the end of the summer of 1861, the situation in New Mexico, from the Texan perspective, looked rather favorable. The immediate threat to Fort Bliss and far West Texas was gone; Baylor's men were now well

Lieutenant Colonel John Baylor, Second Texas Mounted Volunteers (courtesy Jerry Thompson)

Major Isaac Lynde, USA, shown as an old man (Museum of New Mexico, negative #10250)

armed and supplied—thanks to Major Lynde and the U.S. quartermaster; and John Baylor, by his own appointment, was military governor of the Confederate Territory of Arizona.

The *Mesilla Times* reported that the Confederate government was working with "exceeding smoothness, and the valley has not for years been so quiet. . . ." In western Arizona, however, the state of affairs was not so tranquil, as Apaches and renegade Mexicans exploited the redeployment of the U.S. soldiers to make life miserable for the residents of Tucson and the Santa Cruz Valley. It would be several months before Colonel Baylor could spare a company of men to provide some security for the Confederacy's western flank.[15]

But for John Baylor, not even the presence of Fort Craig on the Rio Grande just inside the northern boundary of Confederate Arizona caused much concern. After capturing and interrogating a detachment from the fort on August 23, Baylor wrote his department commander that "there is no artillery at Fort Craig and I could easily take the place but for the jaded condition of my horses."[16] He did go on to say, however, that a larger force would be needed if he had to handle both the Federals and the Indians.

By the time Baylor's letter reached General Earl Van Dorn in San Antonio, the recruitment of a larger force for service in New Mexico was already underway. Brigadier General Henry Hopkins Sibley had arrived in town with orders from Richmond "to organize, in the speediest manner possible, from the Texas troops, two full regiments of cavalry and one battery of howitzers, and such other forces as you may deem necessary."[17]

"Necessary for what?" was, and still is, the question.

Sibley, who had served as a major of dragoons in northern New Mexico, had resigned his commission in the U.S. Army on May 13, 1861, to offer his services to the Confederacy. Forty-four years old and an 1838 graduate of the United States Military Academy, he had fought in the War with Mexico and later served in Texas and the western territories. The major-turned-brigadier was a veteran cavalryman with a somewhat checkered career. He had invented the conical tent and stove that bore his name and were widely used on both sides throughout the war, but he had also been court-martialed (and acquitted) for insubordination during the campaign against the Mormon polygamists. While awaiting acceptance of his resignation, Sibley briefly commanded Fort Union, New Mexico.[18]

Henry Sibley had left New Mexico on June 13 with the parting words to his former comrades, "Boys, I'm the worst enemy you have [now]!"[19] Within a month he had traveled through San Antonio and New Orleans to Richmond, where he explained to President Jefferson Davis how New Mexico Territory's 250,000 square miles were ripe for the plucking. Davis was rather easily convinced and Sibley was soon on his way back to San Antonio with the provisional rank of brigadier general and a mission that has been the subject of considerable speculation.[20]

The written orders given Sibley on July 8, 1861, were simply to raise at least two regiments of cavalry and one battery of howitzers and drive

Brigadier General Henry Hopkins Sibley, CSA
(courtesy Library of Congress)

the Federal troops from the Department of New Mexico. Details were left to the general's "own good judgment."[21] General Van Dorn was directed to "extend every facility" to Sibley, but about the latter's assignment he was told only that Sibley would advise him on that matter upon his arrival in San Antonio.[22]

Major (then Captain) Trevanion T. Teel, one of Sibley's officers who had gone to New Mexico with John Baylor, wrote after the war that General Sibley had told him of plans that went far beyond his written orders. According to Teel,

> The objective aim and design of the campaign was the conquest of California, and as soon as the Confederate army should occupy the Territory of New Mexico, an army of advance would be organized, and "On to San Francisco" would be the watchword.[23]

Teel went on to say that negotiations were to be opened to secure Chihuahua, Sonora, and Lower California. Others have speculated that the capture of Colorado gold fields was also part of General Sibley's grandiose plan.[24]

One cannot help but notice the similarity of the plan described by Teel to the successful campaign of General Kearny some fifteen years earlier. In fact Sibley's proclamation when he entered New Mexico had a familiar ring to it:

> It is my purpose to accomplish this without injury to the peaceful people of the country. Follow, then, quietly your peaceful avocations, and from my forces you have nothing to fear.[25]

Kearny's proclamation of July 31, 1846, had carried almost the same message:

> It is enjoined on the citizens of New Mexico to remain quietly in their homes, and to pursue their peaceful avocations. So long as they continue in such pursuits they will not be interfered with.[26]

Perhaps during his many years in New Mexico and the Southwest, Sibley had become a student of Kearny's Expedition, and perhaps he did have visions of a similar conquest.

But it is interesting that none of the other chroniclers of Sibley's campaign mentions the designs on California. In fact William L. Davidson, another member of the Sibley Brigade, described a very different grand strategy, one that called for capturing the forts in Arizona and New Mexico, leaving a force to hold the territories (say, half a regiment), moving across the Missouri to succor Price, and then joining Lee in Virginia.[27]

The plans related by both Teel and Davidson sound a bit farfetched; but considering what John Baylor had accomplished with fewer than three hundred men, it might have been easy to imagine that General Sibley would do great things with ten times as many.

2

Bloody Valverde

IN LATE JULY 1861 GENERAL SIBLEY BEGAN TO ORGANIZE THE BRIGADE that would bear his name and, when joined with Baylor's command, would become the Confederate Army of New Mexico. Recruited in South and East Texas, the Sibley Brigade consisted of three full, mounted regiments—the Fourth, Fifth, and Seventh Texas Mounted Volunteers—and a quasi-independent artillery unit.[1]

The 810 officers and men of the Fourth Texas Mounted Volunteers were divided among ten companies of cavalry plus one of artillery. The regiment was nominally commanded by Colonel James Reily; however when that officer was dispatched to northern Mexico on a mission to convince the governors of Chihuahua and Sonora to support the Confederacy, command of the regiment had devolved to Lieutenant Colonel William Read "Dirty Shirt" Scurry. This forty-one-year-old lawyer had moved to San Augustine, Texas, from his native Tennessee in 1839. His military career began as a private during the Mexican-American War, in which he had served with gallantry at the Battle of Monterey. After the war he was appointed to the 1858–59 Texas-New Mexico Boundary Commission; thus he was not unfamiliar with New Mexico Territory. He had been editor of the *Texas State Gazette* in Austin, had served in the Texas House of Representatives, and was a delegate to the 1860 Secession Convention where he voted in favor of Texas' withdrawal from the Union.[2]

The Fifth Texas Mounted Volunteers, 835 officers and men, were also divided into ten mounted companies plus a company of artillery. The regiment was led by forty-eight-year old Colonel Thomas "Tom" Green from La Grange, Texas. Like Scurry, Green was a transplanted Tennessean, a Mexican War veteran (also of the Battle of Monterey), and a prominent lawyer and politician.[3]

The Seventh Regiment also comprised ten companies, but only half (companies A, B, F, H, and I) reached New Mexico in time to participate in Sibley's campaign.[4] This battalion of 414 officers and men was commanded by Lieutenant Colonel John Schuyler Sutton. A New Yorker by birth, Sutton had moved to Austin in 1836 and had served in various military organizations since that time. He and other members of the ill-fated 1841 Texan–Santa Fe Expedition had been captured and marched to Mexico City where they were imprisoned for several miserable months during 1841 and 1842.

The final contingent of Sibley's army was a detachment from Lieutenant Colonel John Baylor's battalion of the Second Texas Mounted Volunteers, which had preceded Sibley's Brigade to New Mexico in July 1861. Citing the need for continued Apache suppression, Baylor elected not to accompany Sibley into the northern part of the territory but to remain in Confederate Arizona with the remainder of the Second. In fact one of Sibley's troopers said, "The mountains here are full of Indians and we dread them worse than we do the Lincolnites, by odds!"[5] Command of the 456 officers and men designated to accompany Sibley was assigned to Major Charles Pyron, commanding officer of Company B of the regiment. Pyron, a forty-two-year old Alabama native, was a wealthy rancher from Bexar County who had also served in the Mexican War (like Green and Scurry he too had fought at Monterey).[6]

The Sibley Brigade left San Antonio in mid-October 1861 and straggled into Fort Bliss in December after a difficult seven-hundred-mile autumn march across the West Texas desert. Although disease, desertion, and other causes had depleted the brigade, the addition of the detachment of Baylor's battalion gave Sibley about twenty-six hundred men for his New Mexico adventure.

The Texans' first objective was the Federals' southern bastion of Fort Craig. Established in 1854, this outpost controlled the Rio Grande corridor between Albuquerque and Santa Fe in the north and Mesilla and El Paso in the south and formed the northern access point to the Jornada del Muerto, that dreaded, waterless, ninety-mile cutoff between the Mesilla Valley and points north. Whereas most of the western military posts were built to serve as bases for operations against the Indians, Fort Craig, having been strengthened by the construction of earthworks, was indeed a stronghold for the troops and supplies located there.[7] The capture of Fort Craig was a critical first step in Sibley's overall plan for the conquest of New Mexico. The supplies and forage at the fort were essential to the general's "live-off-the-land" logistics strategy, and the southern wing of the Union army, which was stationed at Fort Craig, would have to be defeated to clear a path northward.

The Union commander in New Mexico was Colonel Edward Richard Sprigg Canby. The forty-five-year-old native of Kentucky and 1839 West Point graduate had assumed command of the Military Department of New Mexico on June 11, 1861, from a southern sympathizer, the one-armed Colonel William Wing Loring.[8] Canby, too, was a breveted Mexican War veteran and had served on the frontier for almost thirteen years. In fact he and Sibley had campaigned together against Brigham Young and the Mormons in 1857–58 and there were even rumors (untrue, as it turns out) that he and Sibley were brothers-in-law.[9]

When war broke out in 1861, there were three regiments of U.S. troops stationed in the Territory of New Mexico—the Fifth and Seventh Infantry and the Regiment of Mounted Rifles. But due to a growing demand for troops elsewhere, Colonel Canby had been ordered to send the regular infantry to Fort Leavenworth, Kansas, and to replace those units with two regiments of volunteers recruited locally. Immediately the newly appointed territorial governor, Henry Connelly, issued a clarion call:

> Citizens of New Mexico, your Territory has been invaded, the integrity of your soil has been attacked, the property of peaceful and industrious citizens has been destroyed or converted to the use of the invaders, and the enemy is already at your doors. You cannot, you must not, hesitate to take up arms in defense of your homes, firesides, and families. As your ancestors met the emergencies which presented themselves in claiming your country from the dominion of the savage and preparing it for the abode of Christianity in civilization so you must now prove yourselves equal to the occasion and nerve your arms for the approaching conflict.[10]

Although neither Canby nor the local Hispanics were enthusiastic about their prospective service together, the call went out, and by January 1862 some four thousand volunteers, including twelve hundred militiamen, had come forward.[11]

Canby dragged his feet on releasing the infantry; and by late February, he had managed to muster almost twelve hundred regulars in the

Colonel Edward Canby, Nineteenth U.S. Infantry (shown after promotion to Major General) (courtesy Library of Congress)

form of three companies of the Seventh Infantry (those that Baylor had not captured at San Augustin Pass), five companies of the Fifth Infantry, three of the Tenth Infantry, two of the First Cavalry, and four of the Third Cavalry. Over two thousand New Mexico Volunteers and another five hundred militia made up the bulk of Canby's command at Fort Craig, while the garrison was rounded out at thirty-eight hundred by a company of Colorado Volunteers.[12]

The First Regiment, New Mexico Volunteers (ten companies) was raised in July and August of 1861. Commanded by the legendary Lieutenant Colonel Christopher "Kit" Carson, the unit was mustered into service at Fort Union by then-Major Gabriel Paul, assistant adjutant of the department. The Second Regiment, also ten companies, was assembled in Albuquerque under the command of Colonel Miguel Pino and Lieutenant Colonel Manuel Chaves. The Third Regiment comprised fourteen mounted companies recruited in September and October at Albuquerque and Fort Union. By late fall 1861, response to the call for volunteers had diminished considerably, and the Fourth and Fifth regiments never grew beyond a few companies each. By February 1862, major portions of all five volunteer regiments had been transferred south to bolster the command at Fort Craig.[13]

Canby was confident that Sibley's objectives included the Federal installation at Fort Union, two hundred miles north of Fort Craig. Although in 1862 northern New Mexico had little to offer a conqueror, political and military control of the north would be a critical factor in any of Sibley's invasion scenarios. Even if the goal was merely a secure corridor to the Pacific through Confederate Arizona, control of Forts Craig and Union and the military forces associated with those installations would be essential. Besides, Sibley would not be satisfied with merely bolstering Baylor's successes—the general needed victories of his own!

Fort Union had been established in July 1851 by Lieutenant Colonel Edwin Sumner, then commander of the Military Department of New Mexico, as a replacement for the departmental headquarters in Santa Fe, a town which he felt to be "a sink of vice and extravagance." This outpost, about thirty miles northeast of the village of Las Vegas, was the westernmost military bastion on the critical Santa Fe Trail.[14] Its garrison provided Indian protection and control over lines of communication both north to Colorado and east to Texas, Kansas, and the Oklahoma Territory.

Fort Union was originally constructed of log buildings immediately below the edge of a nearby mesa. However, when the threat of a Confederate invasion began to take shape in 1861, Canby ordered the erection of a new, more secure installation about one mile east of the original site. Construction of this star-shaped, "bomb-proof" earthwork began in the summer of 1861 and was completed after a major effort in August of that year. As it turned out, the resulting structure was so damp and poorly ventilated that most of the men slept outside in tents or under the stars.[15]

An important part of Canby's strategy was to deny Sibley the logistic benefit of the Upper Rio Grande Valley. Thus he elected to face his Confederate adversary at Fort Craig rather than to mass the Federal forces farther north at Fort Union. This represented a bit of a gamble on the

Fort Union in 1856 (courtesy Library of Congress)

The Fort Union "Star Fort" in 1862 (courtesy Library of Congress)

a Officers Quarters.
b Soldiers do
d Ordance Offices
e Ordance Depôt
f Hospital.
g Dragoon Stable.
h Quartermasters Stores.
i Commissary Stores
k Quartermasters Corral & Shops.
l Bakery
o Offices.
m Laundresses.
p Sutlers.

D

Fort Union

Flag Staff.

part of the Federal commander; Fort Union was garrisoned by only about 550 men, including 250 newly recruited members of the Fourth New Mexico Volunteers.[16] Therefore a decisive Confederate victory in southern New Mexico could have left the rest of the Territory ripe for the picking. Canby must have felt that he would either have to stop the invasion in the south or risk the loss of Albuquerque and Santa Fe with the inevitability of having to defend Fort Union in an all-or-nothing fight.

Colonel Tom Green, Fifth Texas Mounted Volunteers (courtesy National Archives)

Lieutenant Colonel Benjamin Roberts, Fifth New Mexico Volunteers (shown after promotion to Major General) (courtesy U.S. Military Historical Institute)

Sibley finally moved north from his jumping-off point at Fort Thorn on February 7, 1862. By February 16 the twenty-six-hundred-man army had reached Fort Craig where Sibley tried to draw Canby into an open battle. The cautious Union colonel was reluctant to expose his untested volunteers in the open, so he remained near the fortifications and declined Sibley's "invitation." Realizing that he was outnumbered and that his small mountain howitzers were no match for the fort's thick adobe walls, Sibley pulled back a few miles and crossed the icy Rio Grande at Paraje. If Canby would not fight him at Fort Craig, perhaps he would meet him upstream at the Valverde ford.

The ford at Valverde, located a short seven miles north of Fort Craig, had long been recognized as an important military control point in southern New Mexico. In fact Fort Craig's short-lived predecessor in the south, Fort Conrad, had been located just north of the ford and had been relocated only when the swampy environs proved uninhabitable.[17] So when

Sibley crossed the river and moved north on February 20, Canby knew he had no choice.

The Battle of Valverde, the largest Civil War battle fought in the far west, began early on the morning of February 21, 1862, when "Dirty Shirt" Scurry's Fourth Texas Mounted Volunteers and some men of the Second under Pyron engaged in heavy but indecisive skirmishing with a Federal force of regular and volunteer infantry and cavalry and some regular artillery commanded by Vermont-born Lieutenant Colonel Benjamin Stone Roberts.[18] Canby arrived at the ford at about 2:30 in the afternoon, just in time to witness the only lancer charge of the entire Civil War—a glorious but disastrous ride by Captain Willis Lang and Company B of the Fifth Texas against Captain Theodore Dodd and a company of Colorado Volunteers. After surveying the situation, Canby decided to break the stalemate with an enfilade attack against the Texan's left flank with nearly eleven hundred men led by Major Thomas Duncan and supported by a single twenty-four-pounder howitzer. Canby's own left would be anchored to the Rio Grande by six lighter artillery pieces in a battery commanded by Captain Alexander McRae.[19]

Canby's plan was initiated at about 4:00 P.M. when McRae's battery moved forward through the cottonwood bottomland and began to batter the Confederate left. Tom Green, who had been in command of the Texan forces ever since Sibley retired in an alcoholic stupor in the early afternoon,[20] knew he was near the end of his rope. His men and animals were suffering terribly from thirst. He had to slow the Federals' move against his vulnerable left flank, and he had to silence the battery in his front. Looking first to stabilize his left, he dispatched Major Henry Raguet and 250 men of the Fourth Texas to charge the advancing Federals. Then he set about dealing with the battery.

When Major Duncan, in command on the Union right, saw Raguet and his men begin their move toward his position, he stopped his advance and sent an urgent request for reinforcements to Canby. Duncan's excessive caution may have been a factor in the morning's stalemate, and it certainly was a decisive factor in what was about to happen. Canby responded by shifting the four companies of infantry that constituted his center to the right to support Duncan.

Meanwhile Green and Scurry, unaware of Canby's actions across the smoky battlefield, had quickly organized 750 men from the Fourth and Fifth regiments on the Texas right into three waves. Just as Canby effec-

The Final Charge
on McRae's Battery
(courtesy Archives
Division—Texas
State Library)

tively dissolved his center, Green ordered a charge. Within thirty minutes, it was over—Canby's decision, coupled with an unfortunate relocation of McRae's guns near a copse of trees that was quickly occupied by Confederate sharpshooters, permitted the charging Texans to pick off the artillerymen, envelop the battery, and drive Canby's Federals back to the river. The defense of the battery was further weakened by a panicky retreat of some of the volunteers and regulars assigned to protect it.

Realizing that he was in serious trouble, Canby made the decision that probably doomed Sibley's New Mexico campaign and would have profound implications for the Battle of Glorieta Pass to come—he ordered a retreat.[21]

Though the Texans had won the field at Valverde, it was a painful victory and the fruits were meager. Over two hundred men lay dead or wounded, including Lieutenant Colonel Sutton and Major Samuel Lockridge. The supplies and forage at Fort Craig, deemed essential to Sibley's live-off-the-land strategy, were still in Union hands, leaving the Confederate commander with sustenance for only about five days.[22] And to make matters even worse, Canby still had an army of over 3,000 men safely behind the walls of the fort.

3

Marches—North and South

ALTHOUGH "PYRRHIC VICTORY" MAY NOT BE QUITE THE RIGHT TERM, it is clear that Sibley's tactical success at Valverde did little to improve his overall situation. Having failed to capture the crucial supplies at Fort Craig, the Confederate brigadier was faced with the difficult question of what to do next. As usual with such matters, he called for a council of war and, after a lengthy debate, the senior officers agreed that the prospects for forcing the surrender of Fort Craig were not at all bright. The best bet for replenishing food supplies was to move toward the larger towns and Federal supply depots to the north. Accordingly, on the evening of February 23, after the dead were buried on the field at Valverde, five companies of the Fifth Regiment under Lieutenant Colonel Henry C. McNeill led the advance toward Socorro.[1]

The Fifth was relatively well-mounted because of a magnanimous sacrifice made by the Fourth Regiment, namely their horses. Inasmuch as about half of the men of the Fourth had lost their mounts in either the battle or the previous night's stampede to water, Colonel Scurry agreed that it would make sense to convert his regiment to infantry and make the surviving animals available to other units. Convincing the men of the wisdom of that action, Scurry later said, was the greatest victory of his life. Since the horses were private property, the soldiers really did have a choice in the matter.[2]

At Fort Craig, Colonel Canby also held a council of war. The Federals considered three options: (1) they could bring on a second battle; (2) they could abandon the post and try to move around the enemy, impede his progress, and then unite with other forces in the north; or (3) they could hold the fort, await the arrival of reinforcements, and by concerted actions in the direction of the Pecos, defeat the enemy and force his retreat down the Rio Grande.

Canby favored the third and most conservative option and soon had the concurrence of both his senior officers and the Territorial functionaries at Fort Craig, including Governor Henry Connelly. This course of action would keep the valuable supplies at the fort from falling into the hands of the enemy and would leave Canby in a position to interdict any Confederate reinforcements coming up from Texas.[3]

Holding the fort was not the full extent of the Federal commander's plan, however. On the night of the twenty-second, Canby sent out a force of volunteers to operate on Sibley's flank. He also dispatched his quartermaster, a Maryland-born West Point major named James Donaldson, to supervise the abandonment of the posts between Fort Craig and Santa Fe—in particular to remove or destroy all public property that might sustain the Confederate campaign. Several days later, after the Texans had moved out of sight, two cavalry companies, one under thirty-year-old Captain Richard S. C. Lord, and the other under his fellow Valverde veteran, Captain George W. Howland, sallied forth to observe the enemy's movements and communicate with Major Donaldson, who would soon be in Santa Fe.[4]

The first group to leave Fort Craig, a detachment of 280 men under Colonel Nicholas Pino of the New Mexico militia, circled the Confederates and took a position twenty-five miles upstream of Valverde at the town of Socorro. When McNeill and the Texans arrived on the evening of the twenty-fourth, the New Mexicans greeted them with a volley of musket fire. It was a half-hearted effort, however, and when at about 8:00 P.M. Colonel McNeill announced his intentions with a cannon shot, most of Pino's men headed for the hills. Pino himself surrendered at 2:00 the next morning. In addition to numerous prisoners, the Confederates captured 250 to 300 stands of arms, along with much-needed ammunition, horses, mules, and flour.[5]

Continuing up the Rio Grande the Rebels confiscated some corn at Lemitar and then traveled another six miles to Polvadera, the location of a Union supply depot and their next hope for capturing provisions. Unfortunately for the hungry Texans, Colonel Canby's messenger was well ahead of them, and they found the depot virtually empty.[6]

And so for Sibley it was on to Albuquerque, with the fate of the campaign hinging on what subsistence would be found there. Private

Abe Hanna wrote in his diary on March 3, "We are now entirely out of everything in the way of provisions and yet thirty miles to Albuquerque, our promised land." [7]

Hanna did not know it but the Confederate vanguard had reached Albuquerque the day before, only to have their hearts and stomachs sink as they approached the town and beheld three columns of smoke ascending to the heavens. Once again the Federals were a step ahead of Sibley's hapless invaders.

As the Texans would soon realize, however, the smoke was actually a good sign for them. New York-born captain Herbert Enos, an 1856 graduate of West Point and now assistant quartermaster at Albuquerque, had made preparations to remove or destroy all government property, but he had waited until the last minute to complete the task. When Enos got word at about 6:00 P.M. on March 1 that the Confederate advance had reached Los Lunas, only twenty miles distant, he ordered the teams harnessed and ready to move. At 6:30 the next morning he set the fires and headed the wagons for Santa Fe. [8]

The Confederate good fortune came by way of the local citizenry who, recognizing that the Federals were pulling out, stayed up all night waiting for the opportunity to grab whatever the soldiers did not take with them. Since Enos had left the remaining supplies in buildings and fired the buildings rather than the supplies themselves, the Albuquerqueans were able to save a considerable portion of the goods that were meant for destruction. All the Texans had to do was locate what the citizens had carried off and take it away from them.

The responsibility for finding and seizing the supplies was assigned to Private William L. Davidson, a twenty-three-year-old Mississippian and graduate of North Carolina's Davidson College. Until December the former Texas Ranger had served as quartermaster sergeant in the Fifth Regiment. For his efficient work in confiscating supplies "Old Bill," as Davidson came to be known, won the accolades of Colonel Green who called him "the most useful man in the command." [9]

Good news also came from Cubero, the site of another army post about sixty miles west of Albuquerque. On March 3, Dr. F. E. Kavenaugh and three other Confederate sympathizers boldly confronted Captain Francisco Aragon, commander of the post at Cubero, and demanded his surrender. Aragon complied and turned over all property as well as forty-two New Mexican soldiers. Captain Alfred S. Thurmond, in command

Captain Herbert Enos, U.S. Quartermaster
Corps (New Mexico Photo Archives #9826)

of Company A of the Seventh Texas, arrived to take charge of Cubero on
March 5 and promptly sent twenty-five wagonloads of quartermaster,
commissary, and ordnance stores, including sixty muskets and three
thousand rounds of ammunition, to General Sibley in Albuquerque. In
addition, "a citizen carrying public stores" was captured by the Confederate advance guard at Los Lunas.

Captain Enos's trek north from Albuquerque was not uneventful. In a
later report he complained that the train was attacked at the "puebla of
Sandilla [sic]" where six wagons and teams were stolen by "deserters
from the militia or volunteers."[10]

The Federal retreat continued with the evacuation of Santa Fe on
March 4, when Major Donaldson, 200 men, 120 wagons, and supplies
worth $250,000 departed the capital for Fort Union. Again what sup-
plies were not loaded on wagons were set afire, and again some of them
fell into Confederate hands.[11]

William "Old Bill" Davidson, Fifth Texas
Mounted Volunteers (courtesy Archives Division—Texas State Library)

The Federal force that left Santa Fe with Donaldson included Captain Lewis's company of the Fifth Infantry; Captain Ford's Independent Company of Colorado Volunteers; Lieutenant Banks's Company (E), Third Cavalry; two howitzers under Lieutenant C. J. Walker, Second U.S. Cavalry; and some volunteers from the Second New Mexico under Lieutenant Colonel Manuel Chaves.[12]

Things were now looking up considerably for the Texans. When the supplies collected at Socorro, Albuquerque, Los Lunas, Cubero, and Santa Fe were all counted, Sibley figured his subsistence was "ample" and, on the whole, he had sufficiency for some three months. Not only could the campaign continue, but control of northern New Mexico was assured to the extent that the newly won Confederate Territory would need a civilian governor. The appointment went to the former territorial surveyor-general, William Pelham.[13]

On the Federal side there was gloom—even desperation—in some quarters. Governor Connelly, who had hurried north after Valverde, had abandoned Santa Fe and moved the Union territorial capital to Las Vegas.[14] At nearby Fort Union Gabriel R. Paul, now a colonel, wrote on March 11:

> The state of affairs in the Department of New Mexico has been daily growing from bad to worse. . . . All the militia and a large number of the volunteers . . . have deserted. . . . There is a general panic in the country, and people are flying from their homes.[15]

There is no doubt that the presence of the "terrible Tejanos" caused great anxiety among the native Hispanic population; but even so, Colonel Paul's assessment appears a bit exaggerated. Certainly Fort Union was in no immediate danger. Not only had the post been reinforced that very day by a full regiment of Colorado Volunteers, but as one of Paul's newly arrived subordinates put it, the new star fort was so fine a work that "all Texas can't take it."[16]

The Colorado Volunteers, sometimes referred to as Jayhawkers by the Texans, came from an area that had only recently been a part of the Territory of Kansas. The U.S. Congress had created the State of Kansas and the Territory of Colorado at about the same time the citizens of Texas decided to join the Confederacy. Colorado also had its Southern sympa-

Colorado Territorial Governor William Gilpin
(courtesy Colorado State Historical Society)

thizers, and they were at times a boisterous lot, but there was no doubt
that the majority of the territory's population was loyal to the Union.
One test came on April 24 when a Confederate flag was hoisted above a
Denver City general merchandise store. As one writer told it, the thing
was hauled down by Union men "before it had fluttered long enough to
smooth out its creases and wrinkles."[17]

Colorado's first territorial governor, William Gilpin of Missouri,
being eager to furnish troops for the Federal cause, authorized the call
for volunteers shortly after his arrival at Denver City in late May 1861. A
"cosmopolitan" group of hardy, well-seasoned frontiersmen came forward, and by the first of October the ranks of the First Regiment of Colorado Volunteer Infantry were almost completely filled. Barracks for the
First were located just outside Denver City at the newly constructed Camp
Weld.[18]

John Potts Slough, the prominent Denver City lawyer who had recruited Company A, was named colonel of the regiment. Slough, a native of Ohio and former Ohio politician, was not a military man himself,
but he came from a military family. His father had been a general, and
his ancestor Mattias Slough was the first colonel appointed by General

George Washington. The junior Slough would also reach the rank of general, but it would not be because of an ability to inspire troops. His rigid obstreperous nature caused Slough to be generally unpopular with his men. Their feelings seemed to run the gamut from indifference all the way to contempt. One private suggested that the problem may have been his aristocratic style, which savored more of eastern society than that of the free and easy West.[19]

Despite the First Regiment's earlier genesis, two independent companies of Colorado Volunteers that would eventually become part of the Second Colorado Infantry were the first to answer Colonel Canby's call for assistance in New Mexico. Captain Theodore H. Dodd's company was sent to Fort Craig in time to repel the lancer charge at Valverde, and Captain James H. Ford's company reached Santa Fe just as Federal forces there were evacuating the town. The latter unit returned to Fort Union with Major Donaldson.[20]

The First Regiment remained in Colorado until mid-February, when orders were received from Major General David F. Hunter, commander of the Department of Kansas, to "send all available forces you can possibly spare" to reinforce Colonel Canby in New Mexico. Seven companies of the First headed south out of Camp Weld on February 22, the day after Valverde and the day before General Sibley began his march northward.[21]

Lieutenant Colonel Samuel F. Tappan and the other three companies of the First, who had earlier been sent to Fort Wise, near present-day Lamar in southeastern Colorado, departed for New Mexico on March 3, 1862. Tappan, a thirty-two-year-old newspaperman from a strident New York City abolitionist family, had been sent to Colorado in 1858 to report on the Pike's Peak gold rush for Horace Greeley's *New York Tribune*. When the call went out for troops to support the Union cause, Tappan raised Company B and was rewarded with the lieutenant colonelcy of the regiment.[22]

On the evening of March 4, while Tappan was in camp at Bent's Old Fort, a messenger arrived from Fort Union with news of Valverde and an appeal for the immediate advance of the Colorado troops. Tappan relayed the message to Colonel Slough and agreed to hurry forward with his own battalion as quickly as possible.[23]

Colonel Slough received Tappan's message on March 5 while in camp on Dry Creek, north of present-day Walsenburg, approximately the half-way point between Denver City and Fort Union. Slough asked his men if they were willing to endure forced marches for the "honor and prosperity of the Republic," and upon the affirmative answer, the baggage was left behind and the pace picked up considerably.[24]

The lines of march of the two battalions of the First Colorado converged at the Purgatoire River, near present-day Trinidad, on the evening of March 7, and the united regiment continued southward, appropriating livestock and wagons from irate farmers and ranchers along the way.[25] While descending Raton Pass on March 9, the Coloradans were met by another messenger from Fort Union who provided some jumbled intelligence about Texans threatening the fort. The march was accelerated again and continued into the wee hours of the morning until finally, with animals dropping in their harnesses, the regiment was allowed to stop and rest. Assembly sounded at daylight on the tenth and the Federal column moved on, this day to encounter yet more misery in the form of a bitterly cold wind that one diarist described as a gale, and another, a hurricane.[26]

Finally, on the following evening, the cold, hungry, and exhausted Colorado Volunteers marched into Fort Union to a joyous welcome from the garrison, followed by quite dull speeches by Colonel Paul and Governor Connelly. The second half of the march from Denver City had been made in six days, at almost twice the speed of the first half.

The question on the minds of the Coloradans, that neither Paul nor Connelly answered, was, "Where are the Texans?" Slough's boys would probably have been both annoyed and relieved to know that General Sibley and most of his army were still in Albuquerque, with much left to do before resuming the advance on Fort Union. On the night of March 11, Confederate troops in Santa Fe numbered only eighty. The urgency of the situation had been greatly exaggerated.[27]

The reception of the Colorado Volunteers at Fort Union was further marred by the actions of their already unpopular commanding officer. Slough had preceded the column into Fort Union and told Colonel Paul that the tents and supper being prepared for his troops were

> entirely unnecessary, for his men were all mountaineers and accustomed to all kinds of hardships and privations, and that this march was no more to them than a ten mile march would be to the Soldiers of the States.[28]

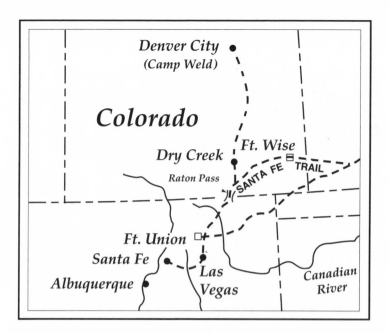

The Route of the Coloradans to Glorieta Pass
Graphics by David Cunnington.

As a result of this magnanimity on the part of the Colorado colonel, coupled with the absence of their supply train with food and bedding, the tired, cold, hungry men were "compelled to lie out all night, exposed to a severe, cold March wind, without a mouthful to eat," a circumstance only slightly improved by "the introduction of three gallons of 'Rot Gut' whiskey to each company."[29]

Back in Albuquerque, General Sibley was still not ready to resume his advance, but the arrival of the Colorado Volunteers meant that he had run out of time for further preparations. Since Valverde the Confederate leader had concentrated on refitting, and he had done that at a rather leisurely pace. Now he would have to shift his attention back to the Union army and the possibility that Canby and Slough would join forces against him—a development that would put Sibley at a serious disadvantage. The obvious strategy for the Rebel general was to prevent the junction and engage Canby and Slough one at a time.

Almost as obvious was the decision to move against Slough first, but to do so in a way that would preserve the flexibility to engage Canby should the opportunity or necessity arise. The plan devised by Sibley called for an advance toward Fort Union by three separate columns. One

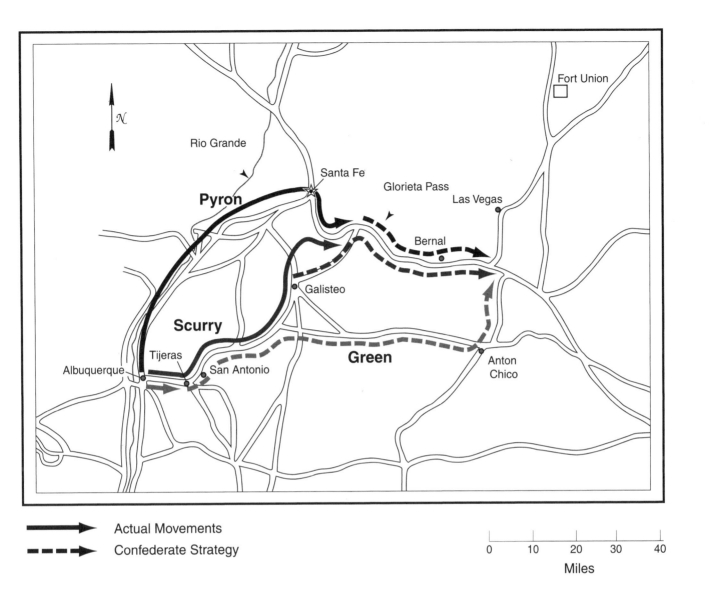

Actual Movements
Confederate Strategy

0   10   20   30   40
Miles

Confederate Advance Toward Fort Union
(Based on an 1864 map of the Military Department of New Mexico
by CPT Allen Anderson as reprinted in Horn and Wallace *Union
Army Operations in the Southwest*)
Graphics by David Cunnington.

under Major Pyron would move from Santa Fe eastward along the Santa Fe Trail and another under Colonel Green would take the southern route from Albuquerque through Anton Chico. The third—and largest of the three—under Colonel Scurry, newly promoted for gallant and meritorious conduct at Valverde, would move to Galisteo. Here Scurry would be in a position to support either Pyron, should Slough be encountered on the northern road, or Green, should Canby be discovered moving up from Fort Craig.[30]

Sibley's plan was set in motion on March 20 when Major John Samuel "Shrop" Shropshire, a twenty-nine-year-old Columbus, Texas lawyer, departed Albuquerque with four companies of the Fifth Regiment to reinforce Pyron at Santa Fe. On the next day Colonel Scurry, in command of the Fourth (minus Company A), and Major Powhatan Jordan's battalion, five companies of the Seventh, took up the march to Galisteo. Colonel Green, with the other six companies of the Fifth, remained near Albuquerque, keeping a weather eye fixed southward. A section of artillery was assigned to each of the three commands.[31]

Captain Thurmond with Company A of the Seventh stayed in Cubero. Captain Hardeman's Company A of the Fourth, along with Captain Walker's Company D of the Second and Captain Bethel Coopwood's San Elizario Spy Company, remained with General Sibley at headquarters in Albuquerque.[32]

Pyron and Shropshire departed Santa Fe on March 25 and traveled fifteen miles east along the Santa Fe Trail to Apache Canyon, where they expected to find forage for their horses, Santa Fe's limited resources having been exhausted. Meanwhile Scurry's lead elements were setting up camp near Galisteo, only fifteen miles to the south. Pyron was to keep moving, while Scurry and Green awaited developments.[33] Scurry, in particular, would not have long to wait.

Since his defeat at Valverde, Colonel Canby's plan had been to await reinforcement from the north and "by concerted operations in the direction of the Pecos and Rio Grande, defeat the enemy and force him to retreat down that river." Colonel Gabriel Paul, in command at Fort Union, had been informed of the plan and was organizing a column to march against the Confederates at such time as he was directed by the department commander.[34]

Major Charles Pyron, Second Texas Mounted Volunteers (courtesy Archives Division—Texas State Library)

Major John "Shrop" Shropshire, Fifth Texas Mounted Volunteers (courtesy Nesbitt Memorial Library)

There was ample reason for Colonel Paul's uninspiring welcome of the Colorado troops. Although he had urged the Coloradans to hasten to Fort Union, Paul's spirits had plummeted when Colonel Slough arrived and pointed out that he outranked Paul by reason of date of commission. This meant that the northern wing of the Federal army, including the column Paul had planned to unite with Canby's command, would be led by this johnny-come-lately from Denver City.

Paul, a forty-nine-year-old West Pointer and battle-seasoned veteran of the Mexican War, wrote the adjutant general in Washington that he was mortified at the idea of losing his command and the opportunity to "reap laurels" to an officer of only six months' service and untried in battle. He went on to request a brigadier general's commission in order to prevent "future such mortifications," realizing that, once again and just as at Valverde, he was going to be stuck with garrison duty while others sought glory on the field of battle.[35]

The Coloradans rested a couple of days before drawing their arms and uniforms, and then they spent an uneventful week collecting rumors and waiting for orders. A message from Fort Craig, dated March 16 and addressed to Colonel Paul, finally arrived on March 21. The department commander's orders were to

> concentrate all your reliable troops until reinforcements from Kansas, Colorado, and California arrive. If in sufficient force to operate directly upon the enemy, advise me of your plans, in order that I may cooperate.

Colonel Canby went on to say, "While awaiting reinforcements, harass the enemy by way of partisan operations . . ." and the message concluded with, "Do not move from Fort Union to meet me until I advise you of a route and point of junction."[36]

Paul showed the orders to Slough, but the Coloradan had already decided to move most of the garrison to a location closer to Santa Fe and he was not dissuaded from doing so by the message from Canby. Colonel Paul objected vigorously by way of two letters addressed to Slough on the morning of his scheduled departure. He suggested that Slough's actions were a blatant disregard of the best interests of the service and the safety of the troops, not to mention the "direct disobedience of the orders of Colonel Canby." And if Slough was determined to go, Paul asked that he at least leave Captain Lewis's command and two sections of artillery to protect the fort.[37] Two days later Paul sent a full account of the dispute to Washington, so as to "throw the responsibility of any disaster which may occur on the right shoulders."[38]

Slough argued that at Bernal Springs, some forty-six miles closer to Santa Fe, he would be between the enemy and Fort Union; and, therefore, the fort would be as well protected as if he were to remain there. He also pointed out that Canby's orders called for the harassment of the Confederates and that could better be accomplished by moving in their direction. Besides, Slough continued,

> if the enemy at San Antonio are no stronger than reported by Captain Walker, the troops under my command will be sufficient to control their action and to defeat them in case of an attack.[39]

Colonel Gabriel Paul, Fourth New Mexico Volunteers (shown after promotion to Brigadier General) (courtesy National Archives)

Colonel John Slough, First Colorado Volunteers (courtesy Colorado Historical Society)

Slough may also have considered the orders out of date inasmuch as they included the phrase "while awaiting reinforcements," and besides, the message was addressed to Colonel Paul, not to him. In any case, at about noon on March 22, Colonel Slough marched out of Fort Union with abounding confidence and most of Paul's former command—including Lewis's battalion and *all* of the artillery—as well as his own First Colorado.

Slough's column traveled twelve miles on the afternoon of March 22, and another eighteen the following day, camping that night at Las Vegas, the territorial capital in exile. According to one Colorado officer, a large portion of the troops spent the first night at the village of Loma "carousing with the Mexican women and fighting with the Mexican men. Some of them fared badly, if we may judge from their appearance the next day."[40] The column reached Bernal Springs after another sixteen miles on March 24, and went into bivouac at a location referred to by Slough as Camp Paul, in honor of his indignant "subordinate" at Fort Union.[41]

While at Las Vegas, Colonel Slough received orders of his own from the department commander. These were a little softer than the orders to Paul dated two days earlier, but it was clear that Slough was on thin ice in terms of obedience. Canby told Slough that with respect to any movement, he must be governed by his own judgment, but if he moved away from Fort Union, a "reliable garrison" must be left behind.

There are at least two other aspects of Canby's orders to Slough that are noteworthy. First there was a set of detailed instructions for equipping his men and packing his wagons—fatherly advice that must have been offensive to Slough as a flagrant recognition of his inexperience in such matters. In addition Canby told Slough he should use mounted volunteers to harass the enemy but the regular cavalry should be kept in reserve. This statement may have had an effect on events to come in a way not considered by Canby when he wrote the order.[42]

To get on with the business of harassing the enemy, Colonel Slough sent Major John Chivington and about one-third of the command toward Santa Fe with instructions to capture or defeat the one hundred Rebels reported to be in the former capital. The rest of Slough's force would remain at Bernal Springs in position to protect Fort Union from any Confederate movements from the south.

John Milton Chivington was born in Warren County, Ohio, on January 27, 1821. Like Slough, Chivington had no military training but came from a military family. His father had been a soldier and his brother Lewis was a colonel in the Confederate army. In 1844 Chivington was ordained by the Methodist Church and served for the next sixteen years in Ohio, Illinois, Missouri, and Nebraska before being appointed Elder of the Rocky Mountain District. Chivington was a huge man—at six-foot-four-and-one-half-inches tall and two-hundred-sixty pounds he was even larger than John Baylor—and he had acquired a reputation for cleaning up frontier towns in the name of the Lord. Once in Platte County, Missouri, when threatened with tarring and feathering if he continued to preach, he stormed to the pulpit and, laying two pistols beside the open Bible, proclaimed, "By the grace of God and these two revolvers I am going to preach here today!" Thereafter Chivington was known as "The Fighting Parson." Chivington proffered his services to

Major John Chivington, First Colorado Volunteers (shown after promotion to colonel) (courtesy Colorado Historical Society)

the territorial governor William Gilpin as an officer in the newly formed Colorado Volunteers in August 1861. He was initially offered a chaplaincy but refused, asking instead for a fighting command.[43]

On the afternoon of March 24, the eighty-eight troopers of Company F of the First Colorado, under Captain Samuel H. Cook, rode another eight miles to San Jose on the Pecos River, where they overtook Captain Howland with three companies of regular cavalry, numbering 150. The 238 cavalrymen were joined by Major Chivington and 180 foot soldiers from companies A, D, and E of the First Colorado on the afternoon of March 25.

The combined Federal force traveled on, arriving at the six-hundred-acre ranch of Napoleon Kozlowski, near the old Pecos Church, late that night. Kozlowski, a thirty-five-year old Polish immigrant who had served five years in the First U.S. Dragoons, no doubt welcomed the Federal troops to his establishment, which included a tavern and one of the last stage stops on the westbound Santa Fe Trail. Lieutenant George Nelson and twenty men of Company F were sent out to search for Confederate pickets, while the remainder of Chivington's command got some welcome rest.[44]

4

Encounter in Apache Canyon

SIBLEY'S NORTHWARD ADVANCE HAD PROCEEDED SLOWLY. IT TOOK two weeks for the Confederate vanguard to travel the hundred miles from Valverde to Albuquerque and another week to reach Santa Fe. Eleven members of Sibley's "Brigands" finally arrived at the capital city on March 10, followed the next day by Major Pyron and another seventy men belonging to the "Arizona Rangers" and Companies B and E of the Second Regiment.[1]

The Brigands were an interesting, if not unique, military unit. They were actually mercenaries on the payroll of Sibley's quartermaster, and they had a reputation for being an unruly set of characters. Alvin Josephy characterized them as "an unseemly pack of frontier gunmen, thieves and ne'er-do-wells who had been collected in the Mesilla Valley."[2]

The captain of the Brigands, John G. Phillips, fit his part perfectly. A native of Ireland and combative by nature, he was somewhat notorious, having made the newspapers in both Santa Fe and Mesilla—the former for participation in a duel and the latter for involvement in a bloody altercation after a community dance. Since the original Brigands came to Mesilla from Santa Fe, the unit was referred to by Sibley's Texans as the "Santa Fe Gamblers."[3]

When General Sibley finally decided it was time to make the move on Fort Union, he sent Major Shropshire with a battalion of the Fifth Regiment (companies A, B, C, and D) to Santa Fe to reinforce Pyron for the march eastward along the Santa Fe Trail. Shropshire reached Santa Fe on March 22 and three days later moved with Pyron about fifteen miles up the road to Apache Canyon, the defile followed by the Santa Fe Trail southwest from the summit of Glorieta Pass.[4]

Separating the Sangre de Cristo mountains from Glorieta Mesa, the western end of the canyon is marked by a narrow passage just east of present-day Cañoncito, while the upper end lies about four miles away, just west of the present-day village of Glorieta. In between, the canyon opens a bit into an area of wooded hills and grassy flats. The deep red soil in the flats is gouged by steep-banked arroyos, one of which carries Galisteo Creek.

On the afternoon and evening of March 25, Pyron's and Shropshire's men set up campsites scattered about the western end of the canyon near a ranch owned by Anthony P. Johnson. Johnson had come to New Mexico from Saint Louis in the 1840s, worked as a teamster at Fort Union, and purchased the ranch in 1858 with four hundred dollars borrowed from one of the officers at the fort. Like the ranches of Kozlowski and Alexander "The Pigeon" Valle, Johnson's Ranch served as a stage stop and way point on the Santa Fe Trail.

Shortly after their arrival at the west end of Apache Canyon, four mounted pickets under Second Lieutenant John McIntyre were sent east through the pass to scout the area around Pigeon's Ranch and Old Pecos. As chance would have it, a group of twenty Federal scouts from Sam Cook's Company F of the First Colorado was also operating in that neighborhood on the night of March 25, and the two parties managed to pass each other without notice.

About daybreak the Federals reached Pigeon's Ranch. This sprawling facility, also known as Rancho de la Glorieta (Spanish for "the ranch in the bower") because of the large number of trees in the area, served as a farm, ranch, stage stop for the Barlow and Sanderson stage line, and Army forage and supply station. The ranch included "corrals, stables, lots, granaries, outhouses, enclosures, water tanks, cisterns, wells, and bake ovens." The inn itself could house and feed thirty to forty people and accommodate several hundred animals.[5]

Alexander Valle, the proprietor and a dedicated Union partisan, nicknamed "The Pigeon" for his characteristic style of dancing, told Company F's Lieutenant George Nelson that the four Texans had passed by and could probably be found a few miles down the road toward Kozlowski's Ranch. One of the Colorado troopers wrote that when Valle found out that the visitors were Pike's Peakers, "he fairly danced, he was so delighted." The Coloradans headed back in the direction of Kozlowski's, and after about a mile, encountered the Texans riding in their direction.

Rather logically the Texans supposed the approaching horsemen were from Pyron's command and asked if they had come to relieve them. Lieutenant Nelson replied, "Yes, we came to relieve you of your arms!" He then turned to his men, said, "Ready!" and twenty rifles were raised and cocked. McIntyre and his three companions threw down their weapons and were marched to the Federal camp.[6]

Major Chivington lost no time in acting on the intelligence gleaned from the prisoners. By the time Lieutenant Nelson and his troopers finished a hasty breakfast, the captured Texans had been loaded into a wagon and sent under heavy guard to Colonel Slough at Bernal Springs, and Chivington had assembled his column on the road to Apache Canyon, three companies of infantry in the lead, followed by Company F and the regular cavalry.[7]

The Federal column gained the summit of the divide at about 2:00 in the afternoon and began the descent into Apache Canyon. Meanwhile Pyron and his eighty men had moved into the upper canyon but Shropshire's battalion of about two hundred was still in camp and some of the troops were asleep. The night had been so cold that "Old Bill" Davidson had not really dozed off until almost noon when the sun was finally high enough to bring a little warmth to his inadequate bedroll. Since neither Pyron nor Shropshire had any way of knowing that their pickets had been captured, they went about business on the morning of March 26 in a leisurely manner, without the slightest idea that Major Chivington was bearing down on them with 418 Federal troops.[8]

The Federal advance guard stumbled into some of Pyron's men just inside the upper reach of Apache Canyon, and the two parties rushed back in opposite directions to sound the alarm.[9] As the report of enemy contact rippled through the Federal column, the excited recruits accelerated the pace, dropping knapsacks, canteens, and overcoats as they hurried toward what was for most the first taste of battle. Within a mile they came to a point where the road bent to the right, revealing a long open space occupied by what appeared to be a company of men with a "red flag emblazoned with the emblem [assumed to be a single white star] of which Texas has small reason to be proud" and two pieces of artillery planted defiantly in the road.[10]

For some reason, Major Pyron had brought two six-pounder field pieces with him, but no artillery officers. It was up to three privates from Company A of the Fifth Texas—William Hume, Adolphus Norman, and Timothy Nettles—to manage the guns as best they could. The cannon were hurriedly unlimbered, and when the lead elements of the Federal column came into view at about four hundred yards, Pyron gave the order to fire. The shells did no real damage, most sailing over the heads of the Union infantrymen, but the firing did disrupt their advance and cause them to crowd together in considerable confusion. It seemed to Private Ovando Hollister of Company F of the First Colorado that the cavalry was plunging wildly here and there, and everyone was talking but not with any purpose.[11]

Major Chivington sent his nervous cavalry to the rear and in fairly short order had matters under control. He sent Company A of the First Colorado, under Captain Edward Wynkoop, a twenty-five-year-old placer miner from Clear Creek and the first sheriff of Arapahoe County, along with Company E, under Captain Scott Anthony, a thirty-two-year-old realtor, into the trees to the left of the field, while Captain Jacob Downing, a Denver City probate judge, took Company D to the right. Captain Cook with Company F and Captain Charles Walker with a company from the Third U.S. Cavalry were dismounted and brought forward to fight on foot. Walker joined the infantry companies on the left, while Cook stayed closer to the road. Captain Howland, in charge the rest of the regular cavalry, was placed in reserve with instructions to charge the Texan artillery in the event it was limbered for retreat. Several smaller parties occupied the center, taking shelter from the cannon fire behind a low ridge.[12]

About to be enveloped by an enemy who outnumbered him more than five-to-one and who enjoyed the advantage of cover on the wooded hillsides, Major Pyron saw clearly that retreat was his only option. He quickly limbered his six-pounders and made a dash for Shropshire's battalion and possibly a more defensible location in the lower canyon. So brief was the Confederate stand in the upper canyon that Captain Walker reported that his troops scarcely got sight of the enemy.[13]

For some unknown reason Captain Howland's cavalry did not charge. As a result they missed a particularly good opportunity to capture the Confederate cannon when Private Norman noticed that a wheel was about to come off one of the carriages and stopped for repairs. Instead of seizing the moment, the Federals imagined Norman was taking a firing position and headed for cover. This delay gave the Texans enough time to secure the wheel and resume their hurried withdrawal down the canyon.[14] A sergeant from Company F of the Colorado Volunteers said

Captain Edward Wynkoop, First Colorado Volunteers (courtesy Colorado Historical Society)

Captain Scott Anthony, First Colorado Volunteers (courtesy Colorado Historical Society)

they mounted their horses when the enemy began retreating but no one
gave orders to charge; the captains and lieutenants just stood around
like "stoughton bottles."[15]

Despite poor aim, the Texan artillery was effective in that it delayed
the deployment of Chivington's force and sent a message to Shropshire's
command that something important was happening in the upper canyon. Hearing the noise, Shropshire's men grabbed their muskets and
without waiting for orders, hurried toward the fray, soon to be met by
Pyron's artillery traveling in the opposite direction at full speed.

Confusion was everywhere as Pyron and Shropshire desperately—
but calmly the men thought—gathered the companies of the Fifth from

The Skirmish at Apache Canyon

(First phase)

Santa Fe Trail

Howland

Downing

Cook

Walker

Pyron

Anthony

Wynkoop

Pigeon's Ranch

Johnson's Ranch

Santa Fe Trail

Kozlowski's Ranch

Miles
0 1 2 3 4

Apache Canyon
March 26, 1862
Approximately 2:45 PM

Approximately 20 Federal Infantrymen

Approximately 20 Federal Cavalrymen

Approximately 20 Confederate Infantrymen

One Artillery Piece

Feet
0 250 500

Contours at 40-ft. Intervals

their widely scattered campsites and formed them into a line of battle about a mile and a half below Pyron's first position. Pyron, the senior of the two Confederate majors, placed his own troops with the artillery in the road and deployed two of Shropshire's companies on either side. The left flank was positioned on a steep, rocky hillock that was described by the Federals as looking like the "bastion of a fort." The right flank occupied the canyonside on the south.

Meanwhile Major Chivington called in his forces, reassembled, and cautiously pressed forward. He pulled up to a point about four hundred yards from the Confederate line, studied the situation, and decided to employ essentially the same tactics he had used in the upper canyon.

Wynkoop and Anthony, with companies A and E, were sent to the left and Downing, with Company D, to the right. Howland's men from the Third U.S. Cavalry, having failed in their initial assignment to capture the Texan artillery, were dismounted and sent to the right with Downing. Lord and his dismounted company of the First U.S. Cavalry joined the infantry on the left. This time Cook's mounted Company F was held in reserve, with the same instructions given to Howland before (although probably in very straightforward no-mistake-about-it-this-time kind of language), namely to charge should Chivington give the order or if Cook observed the Confederates limbering their battery and preparing for a retreat. Chivington rode among his remaining troops in the middle, wielding a pistol and shouting orders. With his six-foot-four-and-one-half-inch frame decked out in full regimentals, the major made a splendid target, but somehow he managed to stay out of the way of the numerous Texan missiles that were no doubt aimed in his direction.[16]

In trying to come into line, Captain Denman Shannon got into something of a pocket, where his Company C of the Fifth Texas was almost completely surrounded by Federals. By the time he fought his way out, at least sixteen of his men had been captured; but remarkably there were no other casualties, although one of the prisoners, Private Perry Sapp, was also wounded.[17]

Early developments in the lower canyon seemed to favor the Confederates, as Company A on the extreme right began to push forward. On the Texan left, however, a serious problem developed. Captain Downing's Coloradans (Company D) had circled the small hill on the Texans' left flank and suddenly appeared in their rear. Pyron responded by ordering the artillery and supporting troops to retreat toward

The Skirmish at Apache Canyon

(Second phase)

Apache Canyon
March 26, 1862
Approximately 4:30 PM

Approximately 20 Federal Infantrymen

Approximately 20 Federal Cavalrymen

Approximately 20 Confederate Infantrymen

One Artillery Piece

0   250   500
Feet

Contours at 40-ft. Intervals

Cook

Santa Fe Trail

Chivington

Walker

Lord

Howland

Wynkoop

Downing

Anthony

Wells

Shropshire

Pyron

Johnson's Ranch

Pigeon's Ranch

Kozlowski's Ranch

Santa Fe Trail

0   1   2   3   4
Miles

Captain Jacob Downing, First Colorado Volunteers (courtesy Colorado Historical Society)

Johnson's Ranch, while Shropshire's men wheeled to the left and formed a new line across a north-facing side canyon.[18]

The maneuver was accomplished, but no sooner was the Confederate left flank reasonably secure than a new problem developed on the right. Because Captain Stephen M. Wells, who had been just a private barely one month ago at Valverde, had pushed Company A of the Fifth Texas forward considerably beyond the main body, he failed to hear Pyron's order for the reverse wheel. Consequently, Company A soon found itself alone and, shortly thereafter, encircled by the enemy.[19]

Major Shropshire, who had commanded Company A until his Valverde promotion, spurred his horse through the Federal lines in an attempt to save his former command from what appeared to be certain capture. Despite these heroic efforts, about thirty of Shropshire's men, including Captain Wells, *were* captured, and Private Samuel Terrell was mortally wounded. It could have been worse, however. Shropshire, like Chivington across the way, drew heavy fire but avoided injury and returned with the remainder of Company A to the Confederate lines. Some of the troops figured they owed their escape not only to Shropshire's daring but also to the fact that the major's presence on horseback in a white hat caused much of the Federal fire to be directed above their own heads. In the words of his grateful troops, Major Shropshire had been "grand, mighty and magnificent."[20] The big Kentuckian seemed to be living a charmed life, but unfortunately this would prove to be only a temporary condition.

Private James McLeary owed his capture in part to a lame leg, the result of a wound received at Valverde. Another member of Company A, Doc Walker, got cut off in a cedar thicket and tried to hide in a hole beneath a large rock. He might have successfully avoided the Federals had it not been that one of his sergeants, Lovard Tooke, was discovered trying to crawl under the same rock. The two men were extricated, and the Federals found some amusement in Tooke's little double-barreled shotgun, which they said indicated that the Texans were on some kind of goose hunt. The levity ended abruptly, however, when Lieutenant William Marshall of Company F of the First Colorado shot himself with the gun while trying to break it over a rock. Both barrels discharged, inflicting a mortal wound to Marshall's midsection.[21]

When Major Chivington saw the Confederates limber their artillery and begin to move backward toward the side canyon, he gave the prescribed signal to his mounted reserve. This time the Federal cavalry responded. Captain Cook spurred his horse to a gallop and Company F charged in a column of twos down the narrow road in pursuit of the Texan artillery. The chase was barely underway, when Cook caught a load of buck-and-ball in the thigh, had his horse fall on him, and then took another hit in the foot. Badly injured, he was forced to relinquish command to Lieutenant Nelson.[22]

The terrain in Apache Canyon was not at all suited to cavalry actions. Arroyos and gullies confined Company F's charge to the rough, narrow road, where dust, smoke, and enemy fire caused many of the troopers, in addition to their captain, to become unhorsed. Several of the riderless horses took the opportunity to desert the army, and it was said that a number of their erstwhile riders bid them good riddance.[23]

Despite the efforts of the Federal cavalry, Private Norman and associates managed once again to escape with the coveted six-pounders. And so with darkness now approaching, Major Chivington decided to call in his troops and bring a conclusion to the affair in Apache Canyon. "Old Bill" Davidson, the Texan who had considered the sun especially pleasant when it appeared that morning and brought an end to a very cold night, found himself wondering later if it would ever set. It almost seemed, he said, "that Joshua had reissued his order to the sun."[24]

The Confederates regrouped near Johnson's Ranch. Some, including George Little, fourth sergeant of Company A, got isolated in the melee and did not make their appearance back at camp until the next morning.[25] Meanwhile, not knowing the status of Scurry's reinforcements and wishing to forestall further conflict, Pyron dispatched a courier to Chivington under a flag of truce with a request to temporarily cease hostilities to allow both sides to recover their wounded and bury their dead.[26]

Some twenty-two years after the battle, Major Chivington wrote that the cavalry charge that afternoon was the most gallant thing he had ever seen—something he had dreamed of as a boy. He went on to tell how the Rebels destroyed a bridge over the arroyo, only to have ninety-eight of Cook's ninety-nine horsemen jump across the fifteen-foot obstacle and charge

> through and through their ranks and back as many as four times, shooting them with their revolvers, clubbing them, sabering them and slaughtering them generally, just spreading destruction among them.[27]

Obviously Chivington's imagination had been at work when he wrote this recollection of Apache Canyon. None of the earlier accounts tells such a story, and casualty statistics clearly belie anything remotely resembling a slaughter.[28]

Sergeant John Miller, who participated in the charge, described the event quite differently in a letter to his father:

> We rode about 800 yards through an awful fire . . . the [Texans] were behind rocks, trees, and there was so much smoke and dust I could not often get sight of one. Seeing that we were in advance of the rest of the company, and there was no battery in sight, we thought it would be foolish to go further through such murderous fire, so we turned to the right and ran up into the hills.[29]

Even so, the drama and glamour of the purported bridge-jumping incident entered the mythology of Glorieta Pass and have persisted to the present in both art and print.

The Skirmish at Apache Canyon

(Third phase)

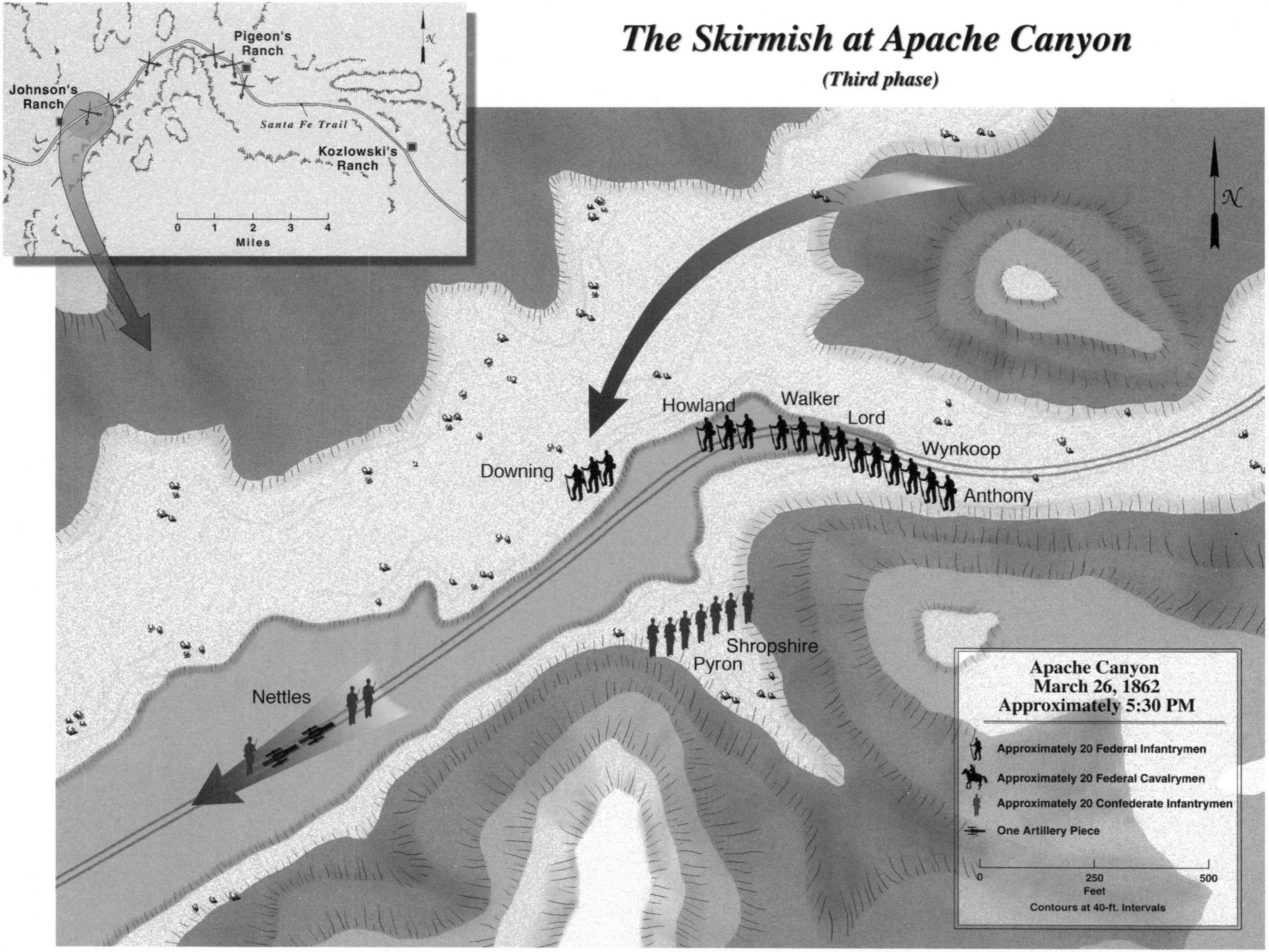

Johnson's Ranch

Pigeon's Ranch

Santa Fe Trail

Kozlowski's Ranch

Miles
0   1   2   3   4

Howland

Walker

Lord

Wynkoop

Anthony

Downing

Shropshire

Pyron

Nettles

Apache Canyon
March 26, 1862
Approximately 5:30 PM

Approximately 20 Federal Infantrymen

Approximately 20 Federal Cavalrymen

Approximately 20 Confederate Infantrymen

One Artillery Piece

0   250   500
Feet

Contours at 40-ft. Intervals

Pyron's Bastion (photograph by Thomas Edrington)

Except for prisoners, casualties were fairly light on both sides. The Confederates lost three killed and one wounded, while Federal casualties were five killed and fourteen wounded. Four of the five Federals killed and most of the wounded belonged to Company F, the unit that made the celebrated cavalry charge.

Prisoners were another matter, however. The Coloradans lost only three; but seventy-one of the Texans, one-fourth of Pyron's entire command, were captured and soon found themselves disarmed and marching under guard in the direction of the stockade at Fort Union.[30]

The First Colorado had fought its first battle and the soldiers considered it a marvelous victory. They reveled in the thought that the "devils from Pike's Peak" had turned back the terrible Texans.[31]

Painting of The Strategic Bridge in Apache Canyon, commissioned by James
Toulouse and painted by Willard Andrews (courtesy New Mexico Archives,
neg. #15188)

In camp at Johnson's Ranch, the Confederates had mixed feelings about Apache Canyon. They figured they gave a pretty good account of themselves, but admitted that March 26 had not been a good day. One member of the Fifth wrote years later that they had been "outflanked, outnumbered, and outgeneraled."[32]

Pyron's big mistake was allowing himself to be surprised. Had he been aware of Chivington's presence, he could have selected a defensive posture that would have compensated for his overall inferiority in numbers—about two-to-three. As it turned out he was never able to get out of trouble. The brief stand in the upper canyon bought time for the retreat and the gathering of Shropshire's command, but the hurried deployment of forces in the lower canyon had some serious shortcomings.

On the Federal side, Chivington's choices were pretty clear. The double flanking maneuver on the upper battlefield exploited both his numerical advantage and the cover afforded by the wooded hillsides. Pyron's artillery was thus deprived of an open field of fire and became more of a liability than an advantage. The same tactics in the lower battlefield were effective again. Even though the numerical advantage was less, Downing's use of the "bastion" to cover his maneuver around the enemy left flank sent the Texans reeling once more.

The employment and performance of the Federal cavalry, however, must be considered questionable. The failure of Howland to charge the disabled battery on the upper battlefield may have cost the Federals in terms of losses two days hence when the guns would be used against them again. Second, despite Chivington's recollections, Company F's charge in column was bound to suffer heavy casualties, and the chances of capturing the artillery on the lower battlefield were modest at best.

5

Interlude

Majors Pyron and Shropshire had worked valiantly to prevent disaster from befalling the men of the Second and Fifth Texas. The two hundred Confederates had fled down Apache Canyon nearly to Johnson's Ranch in relative disarray. Many were separated from their units and about one-fourth of the original force had been captured. During the afternoon Pyron had dispatched a rider to Scurry who, he hoped, was marching north as Sibley's plan required. However there was no chance that the hero of Valverde could help his beleaguered colleagues that afternoon.

Chivington and the Coloradans were also somewhat disorganized. The double flanking maneuver, together with the cavalry charge and pursuit of isolated Texans, left the Federals scattered about the lower canyon. Chivington and his officers recognized that the arroyos in the canyon bottom together with the forested mountainsides made small unit operations risky—a few concealed Texans could easily ambush small, isolated groups of Union soldiers. In addition, they had nineteen of their own casualties to deal with as well as the seventy-one Confederate prisoners.[1]

Then there were the cannon—despite vigorous efforts by the Federals, the three Confederate privates had managed to limber the pieces and move them down the canyon where they could continue to threaten pursuers. So as the shadows lengthened in Apache Canyon, Chivington decided to call it a day. Aides galloped off to Nelson and Downing, and the tired, dirty men of the First Colorado and Third U.S. Cavalry began to collect their dead and wounded and reestablish their prebattle order.

Scurry and 440 men of the Fourth Regiment had set up camp on the Beard Ranch near the village of Galisteo, about fifteen miles south of

Glorieta Pass, late in the morning of March 25. With the arrival early the following afternoon of four companies from the Seventh Texas, Scurry now had approximately six hundred men to assist Pyron in dealing with the newly identified threat from the north.[2] Little did the tired Texans realize how soon this threat would take on calamitous proportions.

As soon as Scurry's men reached camp, foragers were sent into the village to acquire much needed food. They returned with

> a small quantity of corn and a flock of sheep . . . they were naturally very small sheep and were so very poor that many of them could scarcely walk but we slaughtered them and cooked them and ate them with relish. Several of them were old ewes and were near lambing, so near that when many of them were opened up, the lambs that came out of them were able to get up and walk ... still we ate these old ewes and thought they were exceedingly good meat.[3]

Unfortunately dinnertime was to be cut short. Harvey Holcomb of Company F of the Fourth Texas noted: "We began to put our mutton on the fire and thinking and talking about what a feast we would have in a short time and happened to look across the prairie and saw a dust cloud rising."[4]

The cloud that distracted Holcomb and the others from their afternoon lamb feast was Pyron's messenger, galloping across the dry plain from Apache Canyon. The courier reached the Fourth Regiment's camp between 4:00 and 5:00 P.M. and reined to a halt in front of Scurry's tent. Anxiously the men watched the colonel open and read the note handed to him by the rider. The news was obviously not good and one of Holcomb's buddies knowingly remarked, "Hell's a brewing and not a mile off!"

According to Lieutenant Phil Fulcrod, Pyron's message read:

> The enemy has moved from Fort Union and is in full force in my front and we have had heavy skirmishing during the day. I have a strong position. Will hold them at bay and wait your arrival.[5]

Scurry quickly scribbled a response and handed it to the messenger who saluted, grabbed a fresh horse, and galloped back onto the prairie. As soon as he had dismissed Pyron's messenger, the colonel, hat in hand, walked down the line hollering, "Pack up, boys, Major Piran [sic] has

Colonel William
Scurry, Fourth Texas
Mounted Volunteers
(courtesy National
Archives)

been fighting 600 Yankees for two days and has got a truce until 12 o'clock tomorrow and we must go to him."[6] Still chomping on chunks of mutton, the men of the Fourth and Seventh fell into line and were on the march "in about 10 minutes,"[7] leaving the teamsters to break camp and follow with the train as soon as they could.

Scurry had two choices—he could march directly north to Johnson's Ranch, a trip of about fifteen miles, or he could veer east and march across Glorieta Mesa to Pigeon's Ranch, a longer route but one that left him closer to his ultimate goal of Fort Union. Undoubtedly the messenger told Scurry that Pyron was ensconced at Johnson's Ranch. Since it would be reasonable to surmise that the Federals controlled the rest of the canyon, he elected to take the more direct route up Galisteo Creek to Johnson's Ranch.

The road from Galisteo to Johnson's Ranch was cold and snow-covered and many of the men were barefoot. Although some had eaten before their hasty departure, most were still hungry as they trudged along in the cold, dark New Mexico night. Davidson said that he and the others at Johnson's Ranch, on edge after their afternoon fight, heard a deep rumbling late in the evening and, putting their ears to the ground could hear:

> the tramp, tramp, tramp of soldiers on the march. Not the clear ringing of men well shod but some hard clear ringing and others soft, showing sandals or bare feet.[8]

Near the end of the march, around midnight, the men had to climb over a steep grade, dragging the cannons with them by hand. The ascent and descent were so difficult that the last two or three miles took the column nearly two hours.[9]

The exhausted Texans reached Johnson's Ranch at about 3:00 A.M. Some of the men collapsed on the ground to catch a bit of sleep before the inevitable morning fight, while others made fires to try to cut the early spring chill. Still others found friends from the Second and Fifth regiments and pumped them for details of the previous day's fight, oblivious to the opportunity to rest after their ten-hour trek.[10]

Given the darkness, the potential strength of Pyron's defensive position, and the artillery imbalance, Chivington had elected to withdraw four miles to the water and protective adobe walls of Pigeon's Ranch. However the upper battlefield at Apache Canyon represented an excellent forward location so he stationed a reinforced picket line there before pulling the rest of his force back to the ranch itself.[11] Reaching Valle's establishment after about a two-hour march, the tired Coloradans set up a temporary field hospital for the wounded and sent a messenger on to Colonel Slough at Bernal Springs to tell him of the day's events and request immediate assistance.

Pyron's flag of truce passed through the picket line and arrived at

Pigeon's Ranch sometime during the evening. After some negotiation the truce was granted. According to Whitford, some or all of the three Confederate dead were actually buried on the upper battlefield.[12] With the truce established and a strong rear guard set, the men of the victorious First Colorado bedded down for the night, exhausted but exhilarated. Their baptism of fire had indeed become a long day for these inexperienced soldiers and their "Fighting Parson."

Slough responded to Chivington's request for reinforcements by sending about three hundred infantry and cavalry and two cannons under thirty-six-year-old, Welch-born placer miner Captain William J. Lewis, Fifth U.S. Infantry. These troops arrived at Pigeon's Ranch during the night.

The Coloradans had discovered a cache of flour at Pigeon's Ranch, which they readily converted into morning rations shortly after first light on the twenty-seventh. Then looking warily over their shoulders toward the crest of Glorieta Pass, they buried their five fallen comrades "in an open field a quarter of a mile down the canyon" and arranged to send the captured Texans on to Fort Union under the escort of a squadron of cavalry. The eleven wounded men were made as comfortable as possible in a field hospital set up in Valle's house.[13]

Shortly after daybreak on the twenty-seventh, Scurry's seventy-wagon train, which had taken a longer but less mountainous route to the west, began to straggle into Johnson's Ranch.[14] Some of the foot soldiers who had preceded the train the night before, remembering their lamb-feast of the previous afternoon, scoured the wagons in a fruitless search for hidden meat. Coming up empty-handed, the ritual fare of "bread made of flour and cold water" was once again their only meal.

Scurry's initial information had been incorrect; the agreed-upon truce between Chivington and Pyron did not last until noon but expired at 8:00 A.M.[15] So after breakfast, Scurry formed the men into a line of battle across the road leading into Apache Canyon. The Texans stayed on station all day, expecting at any moment to see "thousands of blue-coated Pike's Peakers" round the bend; but none came. After sunset, with a heavy guard set, the men of the Fourth Texas withdrew to Johnson's Ranch for another uneasy night's rest.

Because the large force of men and horses had overwhelmed the water supply at Pigeon's Ranch, Chivington elected to move his command back to Kozlowski's where the water was more plentiful.[16] Early on the morning of the twenty-eighth, Slough and the rest of the Federal force rode into camp.

So the twenty-seventh passed with the two armies reinforcing and anticipating. Neither leader was sure of the strength and location of the other, but each was determined that he would not let another day pass without some sort of resolution. Retreat was not an option for either Scurry or Slough. On Tuesday the twenty-eighth, La Glorieta Pass would be in the hands of either Texans or Coloradans, but not both.

6

Collision at Pigeon's Ranch

THE NIGHT OF MARCH 27, 1862, COULD NOT HAVE BEEN A RESTFUL ONE for anyone in or near La Glorieta Pass, New Mexico. Certainly Alexander Valle, the illiterate forty-five-year-old innkeeper, must have been worried. Seven miles west of his famous "house of entertainment for travelers" on the Santa Fe Trail, at the rest stop owned by his friend A. J. Johnson, were some eight hundred Texans. Five miles east, at Napoleon Kozlowski's ranch, were over fourteen hundred Union troops. There was only one road between Kozlowski's and Johnson's, the Santa Fe Trail, and it ran right past his place of business!

In addition, Major Chivington and his Pike's Peakers had commandeered part of the ranch complex as a hospital for the eleven Union wounded from the skirmish on the twenty-six, and the moans of these men would have been constant reminders of the potential for damage to life, limb, and property.[1]

In the two main camps each of the weary soldiers also realized that major enemy forces were lurking nearby. Neither Scurry nor Slough knew the precise strength of his opponent. Certainly there had been reinforcements on both sides since the fighting on the twenty-sixth. But how many? Scurry accurately guessed he might be facing fourteen hundred men and Slough thought that he faced twelve to fourteen hundred himself.[2] And what about artillery? It was a night of worried frowns and furrowed brows.

Slough and the Coloradans had left Bernal Springs and headed for Kozlowski's Ranch on the twenty-seventh, with the entire command reaching that site between 2:00 and 3:00 A.M. on the twenty-eighth. Because of the perceived urgency generated by Chivington's Apache Canyon engagement on the twenty-sixth, the thirty-four mile march had been an arduous one with but a single halt in nearly eighteen hours.[3]

Chivington had moved his force, including the reinforcements under Lewis, back to Kozlowski's late in the evening of the twenty-seventh. The entire "brigade" was now assembled and, despite it being the wee hours of the morning, when Slough arrived, he had the bugler sound Officer's Call. Tired and dusty, the brain trust assembled—Slough, Chivington, Tappan, Enos, Chapin, and Howland—to decide their next move.

Not knowing the exact numbers or deployment of his opponent, Slough decided to conduct a two-pronged "reconnaissance-in-force" of the presumed position of the Texan forces at Johnson's Ranch.[4] Chivington and about five hundred men would cut across Glorieta Mesa to the Texan rear while Slough moved the main body (almost 900 men) down the Santa Fe Trail to his opponent's front. With the plan decided and orders given, the tired men settled down for a few hours of sleep before what promised to be an exciting day.

Perhaps realizing that the twelve-mile march in mountainous country from Kozlowski's Ranch to Johnson's Ranch with arms ever at the ready would be arduous for his already tired troops, or perhaps because he expected Scurry and his men to wait for him eleven miles away at Johnson's Ranch, the Colorado commander permitted a leisurely morning routine on the twenty-eighth. However, by 7:00 A.M. the camp was stirring, and between 7:30 and 8:00 the regular cavalry mounted and moved out as an advance guard. By 9:00 the entire command was on the road in two columns.[5]

Chivington and his battalion were the first of the troops to leave. They departed at about 8:30 and turned west-southwest on the Galisteo road. Slough's column, led by a detachment of the regular cavalry, possibly commanded by Captain Howland, with Kentuckian Charles Walker's company in the lead, continued north and west along the Santa Fe Trail.[6] Behind the troopers came the infantry, each man with two day's supplies in his haversack.[7]

The foot soldiers, five companies totaling close to five hundred men, were led by Lieutenant Colonel Samuel Tappan, the thirty-two-year-old

Pigeon's Ranch in 1880, looking west
(courtesy Museum of New Mexico,
Wittick Collection)

Denver newspaperman. The infantry was followed by two four-gun artillery batteries. The senior artillery officer, twenty-seven-year-old Captain John Ritter, was a graduate of West Point (class of 1856) and a veteran of the Seminole Wars. He commanded two twelve-pounder howitzers and two six-pounder guns. The other battery, consisting of four smaller and more portable twelve-pounder mountain howitzers, was led by Ira Claflin, a twenty-eight-year-old West Point classmate of Walker's (class of 1857), who had been breveted to captain barely one month earlier for his actions at Valverde.[8]

Ritter's West Point classmate, Quartermaster Captain Herbert M. Enos, and a hundred-wagon supply train, described as "nearly all the serviceable transportation in the department [of New Mexico]," brought up the rear. Because "it was known that the Enemy was in the Canyon beyond Pigeon's Ranch," the young quartermaster had advised Slough not to move the train from the relative security of Kozlowski's Ranch, but his "suggestion was disregarded and the entire train moved forward in the rear of the Command."[9] The train may have been escorted by detachments of the regular cavalry under Captain Richard S. C. Lord and a detachment of the Fourth New Mexico Volunteers.[10] "Believing that a fight would come off," Enos had placed the ammunition wagons supporting the batteries in front, followed by the hospital train, baggage wagons, and supply train.[11]

Twelve miles distant, Scurry and the Texans were also stirring. Anticipating a Federal attack, they had remained in a strengthened defensive deployment since the previous morning. When none materialized, Scurry decided to take the fight to Slough. The men, eating what breakfast they could muster, were told to put the rest of their food into their haversacks and form up.[12]

In standard fashion, the Texans led off with a cavalry detachment, followed by infantry and artillery. Unlike Slough, Scurry elected to leave his supply train, some seventy wagons under the command of thirty-two-year-old Lieutenant John Taylor of Company I of the Seventh Texas Mounted Volunteers, together with his wounded and a small guard detachment, encamped at Johnson's Ranch.[13] This decision, similar to that being advocated by Enos to Slough twelve miles east across the pass at almost the same time, would come back to haunt the Texas commander before the sun set on March 28.

Lieutenant Colonel Samuel Tappan, First Colorado Volunteers (courtesy
Colorado Historical Society)

Scurry's command consisted of about six hundred men. Nine companies of the Fourth Texas Mounted Volunteers, now an infantry regiment, were led by the bearded thirty-six-year-old Nacogdoches merchant Major Henry Raguet.[14] The four cavalry companies of the Seventh Texas were led by Captain Gustave Hoffmann;[15] the four companies from the Fifth Texas were under command of the Apache Canyon veterans, Majors Charles Pyron and John Shropshire. Scurry's vanguard was led by the "Brigands" and the three-gun artillery battery was under the command of Trevanion Teel's Valverde subaltern, Lieutenant James Bradford.[16]

Private Davidson, writing after the war, compared the terrain they were crossing to that of a place in ancient Greece:

> This was a rugged pass between the mountains, Thermopolae [*sic*] was nothing compared to it; steep cliffs of rocks lined thick with cedar brush on each side of the road—cliffs so steep that a man had absolutely to get down and crawl up them.[17]

It is true that the country was rough—by Texas standards, anyway—but there can be little doubt that Davidson's analogy was inspired at least as much by the disastrous events that were about to transpire that afternoon as by the terrain itself.

Scurry's advance guard rode up the winding trail, ever mindful that the Union army could be around the next bend. They passed through the Apache Canyon battlefield, no doubt doffing their slouch hats to the graves of McKinney, Cator, and Terrell, their fallen comrades, and moved with increasing caution to the crest of the pass a mile further on. Passing the crest, they moved down the Santa Fe Trail ever more cautiously until they reached a point about a mile west of Pigeon's Ranch.

Suddenly the Texan vanguard heard unmistakable sounds indicating the presence of a major force a short distance to their front. Not wanting to bring on an engagement without sufficient forces, the cavalrymen quietly withdrew into the woods and sent for Colonel Scurry. As soon as the messenger arrived, Scurry hastened to the front. He ordered the troopers to "retire slowly to the rear, dismount, and come into action on foot."[18]

Word was passed back to unlimber the artillery in the road on a small rise and for the infantry to deploy in a single line of battle across

Major Henry Raguet, Fourth
Texas Mounted Volunteers
(courtesy Gary Hendershott)

the Santa Fe Trail. Sergeant Alfred Peticolas of Company C of the Fourth
Texas described the terrain that lay before him:

> The road here . . . runs through a densely wooded pine country where
> you cannot see a man 20 steps unless he is moving. The hills slope up
> from the valley gradually, rising more abruptly as they near the moun-
> tains. Heavy masses of rock, too, crown most of the hills, and the tim-
> ber is low and dense. On the left [north], the hills rise more abruptly
> than on the right and the rocks are larger. About a mile down the can-
> yon is Pigeon's Ranch, around which was the enemy's encampment.[19]

Scurry's initial deployment placed Pyron on the far right with
Shropshire's four companies of the Fifth just to his left. Raguet commanded the center and left with the nine companies of the Fourth plus
Bradford's artillery; and Scurry himself took charge of the far left with
the four companies of the Seventh.[20] However, this parade ground organization, to the extent that it ever existed, was soon in disarray because

of the nature of the ground and, as Davidson told it, "the companies and men got all mixed up before we had been fighting very long."[21]

The slow westward advance of the Union forces from Kozlowski's Ranch had been relatively uneventful. Chivington and his column flanked to the west shortly after 8:30 A.M., and the rest of the column trudged on. Howland and the advance guard reached Pigeon's Ranch at about 9:30. No doubt the hospital stewards were glad to see the troopers and reported that they had noted no rebel activity in the area. Stationing pickets around the western edge of the ranch, Howland dismounted the men, probably sending a messenger back to the main column to tell Slough, Tappan, and the others that the ranch appeared to be secure.

Not far behind the advance guard, Tappan and the infantry rounded the bend and saw the main ranch house with its long porch, gabled roof, and multiple chimneys nestled in a small grove of cottonwood trees.[22] Marching beside the split rail fence that lined a field east of the complex, Tappan realized that this was the last opportunity for water before they met the Texans at Johnson's Ranch and gave the orders for the men to fall out, stack arms, and top off their canteens. Having marched nearly nonstop from Denver to Fort Union and Fort Union to Glorieta, these men did not need to be told twice to stop marching! Soon the column turned into semiorganized pockets of soldiers starting fires for coffee, with their muskets neatly stacked nearby.

Meanwhile the batteries and train continued to come up. Enos, still reluctant to place the train at risk, identified a location about one mile east of Pigeon's to park the train. Riding forward to find Slough at about 9:45, he requested permission to park the train in this location. Slough did not object to the location but "thought it was not best to park the train yet," so the wagons continued their slow advance, with the head of the train reaching the ranch just before 11:00 A.M.[23]

After reaching the ranch himself at about 10:30, Slough decided to send a detachment of cavalrymen up the road to "reconnoiter the position of the enemy." He directed his thirty-one-year-old acting assistant adjutant general, Captain Gurden Chapin of the Seventh U.S. Infantry, to lead the detachment, which consisted of Captain Walker and elements of the regular cavalry.[24] Chapin and several other regular army officers may have had some special concerns as they left the ranch, moving west. Their wives, along with the wife of Colonel Canby himself, were in Santa

Some Officers of the Colorado Volunteers. Back row: Captain Silas Soule, Captain James Shaffer, Captain Samuel Cook. Front row: Captain Samuel Robbins, Dr. John Hamilton, MD, Major Edward Wynkoop, Colonel James Ford (courtesy Colorado Historical Society)

Fe—thirty miles inside Confederate-controlled territory![25] The men mounted up and rode out of the ranch and down the road, soon disappearing into the pine trees.

The Federal cavalry had progressed less than half a mile when their outriders encountered Scurry's advance guard. According to Davidson, one of the Union troopers called out, "Get out of our way, you damned sons of bitches, we're going to take dinner in Santa Fe!" To this Private Thomas Kirk of Company D of the Fourth Texas Mounted Volunteers shouted back, "You'll take dinner in Hell!"[26] The two sides had finally met in force—the battle was joined! It was now a few minutes before 11:00 in the morning.

Bradford's three artillery pieces immediately opened on the approaching Union troops. Chapin dispatched a courier back to Slough and sent Walker and the rest of the cavalrymen, now dismounted, scurrying for cover into the woods south of the road. Sergeant Peticolas wrote that the fight immediately assumed the form of a skirmish, with men behind the rocks and trees, "we began to fire at intervals with our minié muskets as we could see an object to fire at."[27]

Back at Pigeon's Ranch, one of the Colorado company commanders noted,

> the men were scattered about promiscuously, unconscious of danger, unprepared for an attack, all believing our pickets far in advance; the officers lounging about, the men gaily laughing, singing, and chatting of the past, when, like the terrible storms of the tropics, there burst upon our startled ears, no more than four hundred yards in advance, the deafening roar of artillery.[28]

Lieutenant Colonel Tappan was the first to respond, ordering the batteries and their infantry supports forward. Ritter and Claflin moved about four hundred yards up the road at the double quick, deployed the batteries, and called for Enos to bring up the ammunition wagons. Ritter's battery, supported by Captain Richard Sopris of the First Colorado Volunteers, unlimbered to the right in the road, and Claflin, supported by Captain Samuel Robbins and Company K of the First Colorado, set up to the left.

Walker and Chapin realized that they could not hold their position without help, and fortunately that help was not long in coming. Slough, "having by now recovered part of his equilibrium" and using "language anything but courteous,"[29] ordered the regiment's color company, Company D under Captain Jacob Downing, to move to the left as skirmishers in support of Walker's beleaguered troopers. Slough also ordered Company I, now led by Lieutenant Charles Kerber in place of Captain Charles Mailie, to swing around and flank the Texans' left. Downing, fearing that this move led by the ever-conspicuous color bearer would "bring upon his company the fire of four-fifths of the enemy's command," arrived on the left just as the Union batteries opened fire. The erstwhile probate judge's fears were soon allayed, however, and he reported that "all were actively engaged in the pleasant amusement of shooting rebels." As soon as Ritter's guns opened, Walker was ordered to mount and follow Slough to the rear.[30]

Meanwhile Kerber and his company of German-Americans had found a ravine that ran roughly east–west in a field north of the Texan position. Apparently believing that they could sneak past the enemy flank undetected and attack the annoying artillery, they set out around the Texan left.

Unfortunately for Kerber and his men, Scurry's troops had detected their movement. Mustering a mixed force of the Seventh and Fourth, the Texans leapt a fence and ran two hundred yards across a cleared field toward the gully. Crossing the field exposed the men to heavy fire from both Kerber's company in the ravine and the Coloradans in and around the batteries, but the Texans managed to reach the ravine where a ferocious fight ensued. Davidson characterized it as the "best stand [the Federals] made all day," noting that Captain Charles Buckholts, commander of Company E of the Fourth Texas and a thirty-eight-year-old Galveston lawyer, "after emptying his pistol at them, killed two with his knife."[31]

Three privates described the participation of Ben White of Company C of the Fourth Texas in the fight for the ravine:

> He took a handful of powder, poured it into one barrel of his gun, took another handful, poured it into the other barrel, put a little paper on it and rammed it down and then poured a handful of shot in each barrel, ran a little paper down and turned both barrels loose right down that ravine and killed and wounded at least ten of them and scared the balance of them to death. We reckon they thought an earthquake had struck them. We charged the gully and they skedaddled but we think that Ben White's old *swie*-barrel gun did the balance.[32]

The fighting in and about the gully raged for about half an hour, but Kerber was badly overmatched. Company I suffered fifteen killed, twenty wounded, and five prisoners—nearly 50 percent casualties—an appalling introduction to battle for men who had never "seen the elephant."[33] Finally Company I, or rather what was left of it, beat a hasty retreat back toward the ranch, leaving their dead and wounded behind.

One of those left behind for dead, Lieutenant John Baker, had fallen just as he attempted to lead a charge on the Texan artillery. His body was later found up the hillside where he had apparently dragged himself after Company I withdrew. Though terribly wounded, he had managed to start a small fire to ward off the chill. Unfortunately someone found him

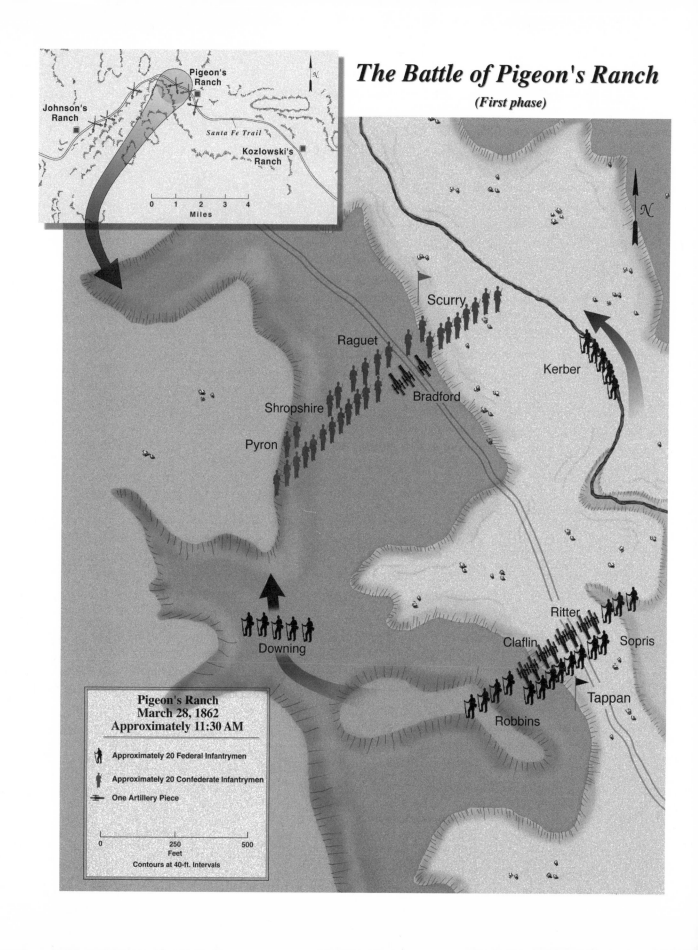

The Battle of Pigeon's Ranch

(First phase)

Johnson's Ranch

Pigeon's Ranch

Santa Fe Trail

Kozlowski's Ranch

0 1 2 3 4
Miles

N

N

Scurry

Raguet

Kerber

Shropshire

Bradford

Pyron

Ritter

Claflin

Sopris

Downing

Tappan

Robbins

Pigeon's Ranch
March 28, 1862
Approximately 11:30 AM

Approximately 20 Federal Infantrymen

Approximately 20 Confederate Infantrymen

One Artillery Piece

0 250 500
Feet
Contours at 40-ft. Intervals

before his comrades could rescue him because when they reached his pitiful "campsite" the next morning they found that he had been "beaten to death with the butt of a musket or club and his body stripped of its clothing . . . his head [was] scarcely recognizable, so horribly mangled."[34] Ovando Hollister, the Colorado chronicler, later suggested that this was done by some "miserable Greasers," not by the Texans.[35]

On the Union left, Downing and Company D were also heavily engaged. Initially they were able to harass Bradford's battery support forces, but shortly the batteries redirected their fire toward the Union skirmishers in the woods and "the whistling of grape, the falling of limbs, the low cry of some brave fellow, for some time was all that was heard."[36] The "pleasant amusement of shooting rebels" had turned into serious business as the Texans began to counterattack. Under this onslaught, which led to the majority of the forty-two casualties suffered by Downing's men that day, Company D fell back about a hundred yards to the protection of a thicket where they collected their forces and offered some resistance to Pyron's advance. Pyron had now begun to extract revenge for what Downing had done to him two days earlier at the "bastion" in Apache Canyon. Lieutenant Eli Dickinson and his platoon of Company D fell all the way back to one of the artillery batteries where he found Robbins and Claflin standing together with Robbins acting as a cheerleader, laughing aloud and cheering, "Ha! Ha! Claf, you're a brick!" whenever the Union artillery struck home.[37]

Meanwhile Captain Ritter was having some trouble finding the right spot for his battery. After firing a number of rounds from his initial position, he was ordered to move south of the road and back toward Pigeon's Ranch. Here, exposed to galling fire and supported by only one platoon of infantry, the captain took it upon himself to move to a third position back on the road. After Lieutenant Peter McGrath was fatally wounded, Ritter moved the battery again, this time to a location directly in front of Pigeon's Ranch. Despite his problems, Ritter extracted a toll on the Texans. In addition to wounding Lieutenant Bradford, Scurry's chief artillerist, the accurate firing of Private Kelly and his batterymates had struck one of the Texan howitzers full in the muzzle and had blown up a limber box.[38] This counterbattery effort temporarily silenced the Confederate artillery and gave a welcome respite to the men on the Union left who were suffering at its hands.

Since there were no other artillery officers in the area, a decision was made, unbeknownst to Scurry, to withdraw the battery completely, and the Texas artillerymen "cut out the horses that had been killed, hastily limbered up, and departed."[39] Fortunately for the Texans, the Federals were still reeling from the blows on the left and right and were unable to capitalize on this potential weakening in the center of the Texan line.

It was now about noon and given the casualties to companies I and D on the Union side and the loss of the Texan battery, it had been an eventful hour. As Slough repositioned and Scurry tried to find his artillery, a lull ensued, punctuated by only an occasional minié ball whizzing overhead.

7

Confederate Victory

COLONEL SLOUGH, EAGER TO SHAKE THE IMAGE OF A NEOPHYTE, had lost no time in taking the offensive in this first battle of his military career. He had opened with the double flanking maneuver that had worked well for Chivington two days earlier, but that particular move failed miserably for him. Now badly bloodied—at least insofar as the two companies that carried the fight to the Texans were concerned—the Federal commander sought a defensive position that would take advantage of the buildings and corrals at Alexander Valle's sprawling ranch.

Attempting to exploit his considerable advantage in artillery, Slough placed Captain Ritter's four pieces near the road where they would most likely oppose Scurry's two remaining guns, and he sent Claflin with his four mountain howitzers to the top of a low wooded hill just across the road and south of the ranch. Captain Downing's battered Company D was ordered to join Sopris's Company C in support of Ritter, and Company K under Robbins was sent to the left to support Claflin.[1]

Company F, the cavalry unit of the First Colorado, was dismounted, split, and sent to the flanks. A detachment took positions on the hill on the south (where Claflin had his battery), while Lieutenant Nelson, who had replaced the seriously wounded Sam Cook as company commander, moved with the remainder to a narrow rocky ridge that projected from the hillside just north of the ranch. Captain Wilder's Company G and the regular cavalry remained in reserve.[2]

Colonel Scurry did not pursue the retreating Federals immediately, but took some time to gather his forces and plan his attack. The Federals had pulled back to Pigeon's Ranch about noon; it was almost an hour later when Scurry renewed the fray.[3]

So well concealed were the Federals that Scurry was not sure whether they had taken cover at the ranch or behind a ledge of rocks beyond. In any case, the Confederate commander sent Major Shropshire into the trees on the right to find and attack the Federal left flank and dispatched Major Raguet to the left with corresponding orders. While awaiting developments on the flanks, Scurry sought out the enemy himself by probing with his two cannons, which had been brought back to the front under the command of Sergeant John W. Patrick and Private William D. Kirk. Once the flanks were engaged, Scurry intended to lead a charge against the middle.[4]

To bolster the Federal left, Slough sent Lieutenant Colonel Tappan with twenty men from Company C, together with his police guard (another seventy), to form a skirmish line along the hill on the south, below and to the left of Claflin's battery. The Federal line now began to take the shape of a fishhook—the eye on the ridge north of Pigeon's, the shank in front of the ranch, and the curve bending around the hill on the south.[5]

Besides being a strong defensive position, the hill provided a point for observation of Confederate movements. When Tappan saw Scurry massing what appeared to be between two hundred and three hundred men for an attack against the Federal center, he relayed the intelligence to Colonel Slough, who quickly repositioned Claflin and his four guns from the hilltop to the canyon alongside Ritter. Tappan was ordered to hold the hill at all hazards and be ready to attack the enemy flank when Slough charged the front. Slough would strike when Major Chivington attacked the Confederate rear, "which he expected every moment."[6]

The Federal forces on the hill occupied high ground with particularly good cover provided by the trees and large boulders. It was the Union right flank that would be the key to the battle, and both sides seemed to be recognizing that fact as Scurry sent Major Pyron to assist Raguet on the Confederate left, and Slough moved three platoons—one each from Company C under Lieutenant Chambers, Company D under Captain Downing, and Company G under Captain Wilder—to reinforce Lieutenant Nelson on the rocky ridge.[7] The other platoon of Company G, under Lieutenant Hardin, supported the batteries, which now enjoyed a four-to-one advantage over the Texan guns in the artillery duel in the center.

Fighting resumed briskly enough on the Confederate left but sporadically on the right. The thick trees on the hill south of the ranch reduced the conflict there to "a sort of bushwhacking," as Colonel Slough put it. Discouraged by deadly fire from the well concealed Coloradans,

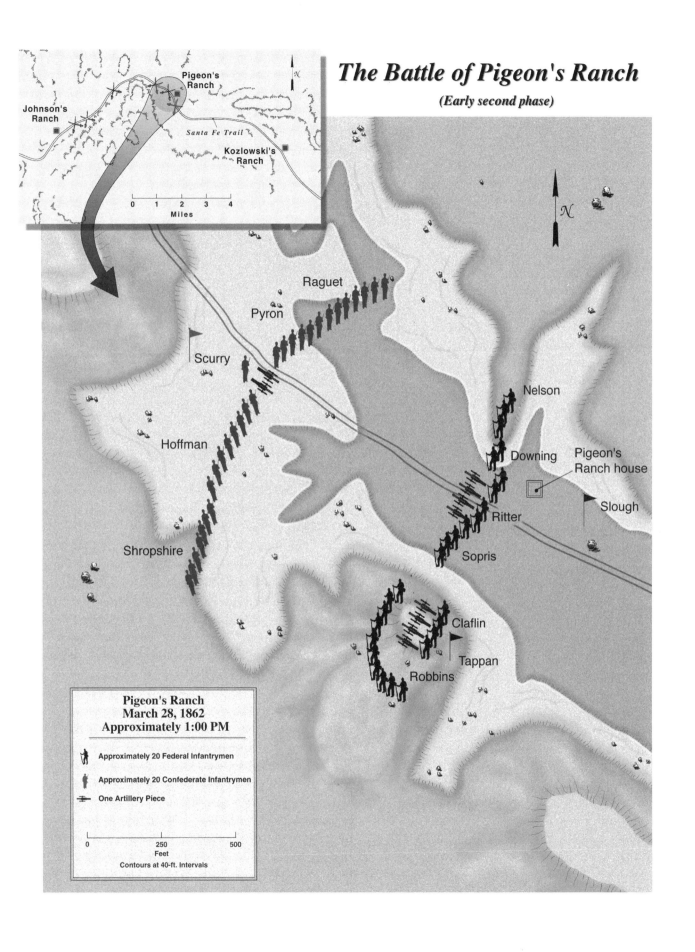

The Battle of Pigeon's Ranch
(Early second phase)

Pigeon's Ranch

Johnson's Ranch

Santa Fe Trail

Kozlowski's Ranch

N

0 1 2 3 4
Miles

Raguet

Pyron

Scurry

Hoffman

Shropshire

Nelson

Downing

Pigeon's Ranch house

Slough

Ritter

Sopris

Claflin

Tappan

Robbins

N

Pigeon's Ranch
March 28, 1862
Approximately 1:00 PM

Approximately 20 Federal Infantrymen

Approximately 20 Confederate Infantrymen

One Artillery Piece

0   250   500
Feet
Contours at 40-ft. Intervals

the Texans had to be goaded a bit by their officers to press on. As Company B of the Seventh fell back in disorder after failing to take a rock ledge, Major Shropshire came up with seven or eight soldiers from Company A of the Fifth (his old company, now under the command of Sergeant James M. Carson[8]) and hollered to Company B to come on and help take the position, or stay back and watch men that would.[9]

After issuing that challenge, Shropshire climbed down off his horse, slipped his arm through the reins, and started toward the enemy position. He was about ten yards away when a Colorado private named Pierce fired a musket ball that struck him in the forehead, killing him instantly. Taken aback by the sudden loss of their inspirational leader, the Texans fell back and took cover in a gully to the left of the rock ledge.[10]

The relative quiet on the right prompted Colonel Scurry to push his horse in that direction to investigate the delay. What he found was disheartening. Not only had no progress been made, but three valued officers and at least three men had been lost. In addition to Shropshire, Captain Buckholts of Company E of the Fourth Texas had been killed "by a saber thrust," and Captain Denman Shannon of Company C of the Fifth (Shropshire's Battalion), who had narrowly escaped capture on the twenty-sixth, had been captured by the same Private Pierce who had killed the major.[11] Scurry called off the attack on the right flank and returned to the canyon to exploit the more favorable results on his left.[12]

Not all of the Texans on the right were aware of either Shropshire's death or Scurry's orders to fall back. Sergeant Peticolas, for one, presumed that Shropshire had been successful and continued forward to his own abrupt encounter with the enemy. Peticolas, on the extreme left of the Texan right wing, discovered that he could participate in the fight in the center by shooting down on the Federal artillery in the valley. After firing a half dozen shots, Peticolas moved farther along the hillside and stopped to reload. Glancing sideways, he found himself within a matter of feet of "100 . . . strangers." Peticolas's heart raced and his arm continued ramming as he desperately considered his options at this unfortunate turn of events.

Capture, Peticolas thought, was certainly preferable to minié balls or bayonets, but before he could say anything, Lieutenant Colonel Tappan of the First Colorado offered some advice, "You had better look out, Captain, or those fellows will shoot you."[13] That of course was what Peticolas was afraid of, but realizing that there were two kinds of fellows about, he replied with a question, "Who will?"

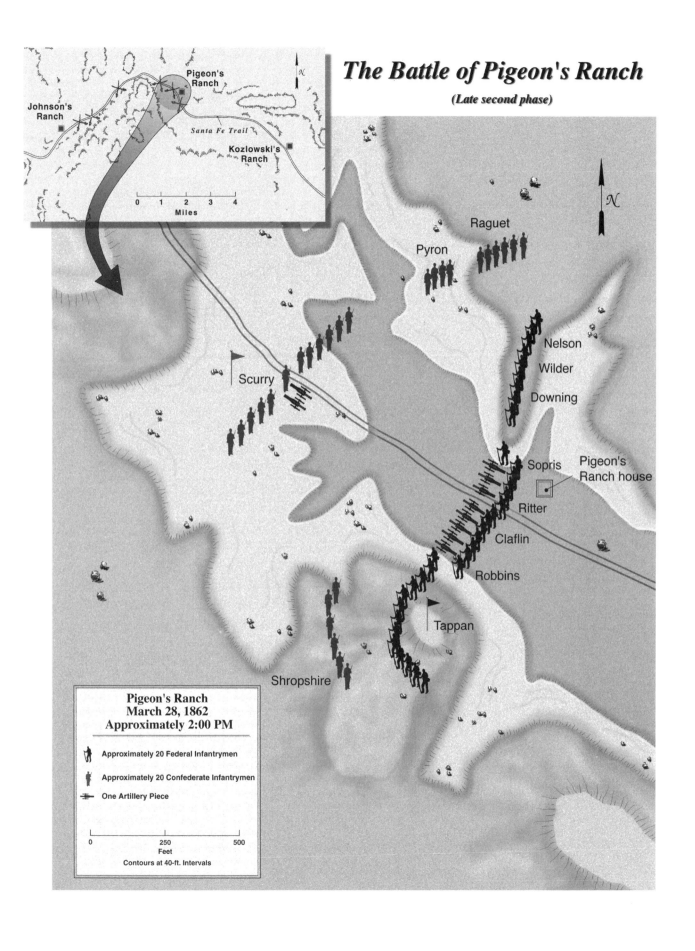

The Battle of Pigeon's Ranch
(Late second phase)

Johnson's Ranch

Pigeon's Ranch

Santa Fe Trail

Kozlowski's Ranch

0 1 2 3 4
Miles

N

Raguet

Pyron

Scurry

Nelson

Wilder

Downing

Sopris

Pigeon's Ranch house

Ritter

Claflin

Robbins

Tappan

Shropshire

Pigeon's Ranch
March 28, 1862
Approximately 2:00 PM

Approximately 20 Federal Infantrymen

Approximately 20 Confederate Infantrymen

One Artillery Piece

0   250   500
Feet
Contours at 40-ft. Intervals

Captain Denman
Shannon, Fifth Texas
Mounted Volunteers
(courtesy Jay
Matthews, Jr.)

"Why those fellows over yonder," said Tappan, pointing in the direction of some Texans who had been taking pot shots at the Coloradans on the hill. Peticolas then coolly declared that in that case he would "go over that way and take a shot at them."

In no time at all, Peticolas was out of sight, giving thanks to "an overriding Providence" for his escape. He might also have given thanks for the confiscated Federal coat that he wore—the one that looked just like those issued to the Colorado Volunteers at Fort Union.[14]

It was now about 2:30 in the afternoon. Shropshire's attack on the right had failed and Raguet's progress on the left was slow, but the pressure on the flanks had at least drawn some of the infantry support away from Ritter's and Claflin's artillery in the middle. Colonel Scurry, again running low on patience, decided it was time to test the Federal center. As Captain Downing of the First Colorado reported:

> Then came the grandeur of battle, the test of bravery, the madness of despair. With wild, fierce yells that reached far above the roar of artil-

lery, in solid column, on they came, while six- and twelve-pound howitzers hurled their double charges of grape and canister among them with a precision which proved most terrible; but unchecked, this mass of excited humanity rushed fearlessly on.[15]

Captain Ritter, whose artillery was the object of the charge, reported more concisely, "The enemy here made a desperate charge on the batteries."[16]

Downing went on to say that just when the prize was within the Texans' grasp, the infantry supports (some of which he commanded) sprang up,

> like tigers from their lairs [and] sent their minié messengers among the Texans, which made them halt before the flashing bayonet, turn and run, when such shouts from the Colorado boys rang along the canyon as were never heard before.

According to the less dramatic Ritter, the enemy "was repulsed with, I think, great loss."

In any case, the Confederate effort against Slough's center failed. Scurry's hope now rested on Raguet and Pyron and the contest for Sharpshooter's Ridge, the rocky prominence that commanded Pigeon's Ranch on the north.

The ridge was ideal for defending against an attack from the west. That side, as well as the narrow southern face, are essentially vertical. The eastern slope is moderate enough to allow ready access to the defender, and the weathered sandstone at the top of the ridge served as ready-made battlements. A successful attack would have to come from the north, but even on that side the rocks and trees provided strong defensive positions.

Progress on the left had been slow for the Texans but it had also been comparatively steady. By mid-afternoon Raguet and Pyron had succeeded in flanking Sharpshooters Ridge and now they were beginning to push onto the prominence itself. The detachments from companies C, D, F, and G of the First Colorado Volunteers made a valiant effort to hold their critical position, but the Texans kept coming and soon were in position to direct a downward fire on the Federal artillery as well as the stubborn infantry who were still resisting from the slope below.[17]

With this turn of events, the situation had changed dramatically.

Once the Confederates occupied Sharpshooters Ridge, the Federal dominos began to fall. Captain Ritter's battery was especially vulnerable to the enfilade fire from above. When a second draft horse was killed, Ritter decided he had better fall back while he still had the horsepower to take his guns with him. By then one of his cannoneers had been killed and another three wounded.[18]

Claflin, taking a cue from Ritter, also limbered his guns and headed toward the rear. Some of Robbins's men helped with a broken carriage and the infantrymen quickly fell in behind. In a situation eerily reminiscent of Valverde, a large gap now existed between units on the Union left and right. As the Texans advanced behind the retreating Federal center, the Coloradans on the right, under Chambers, Downing, Nelson, and Wilder, were all but surrounded. Downing, the senior captain, gave the order to fall back, and with the notable exception of Lieutenant Chambers, who was severely wounded in the shoulder and leg, most of the would-be defenders of Sharpshooter's Ridge were able to make their escape.[19]

The Federal left was in a similar predicament, if a somewhat less serious one. From his vantage point on the hill Lieutenant Colonel Tappan watched the Confederates pour down the road on his right and began to have visions of his own capture. Tappan's orders had been to "hold the hill at all hazards" and attack the Confederate flank when Slough charged the front. Certainly Slough was not attacking, so even though he had an opportunity to do the Texans some damage, Tappan elected to withdraw by way of a "circuitous route" to the south to a point about two miles beyond the present conflict.[20]

Colonel Slough was ready to throw in the towel, but he realized that the situation could go from bad to much worse if he did not make one more stand. He had to buy enough time to get his wagon train underway before he gave the order for a general retreat.

Captain Enos had been fretting about the security of the hundred-wagon supply train all day. In fact he could not understand why Slough brought the train along in the first place. It would have been much wiser, he thought, to have left all but the ammunition and hospital wagons well to the rear of any potential conflict.[21] But Slough rejected the suggestion, and the train had followed the Federal column along the Santa Fe Trail, reaching Pigeon's Ranch just as the battle opened. Enos had hurriedly turned the train around but, again, Colonel Slough overruled Enos's wish

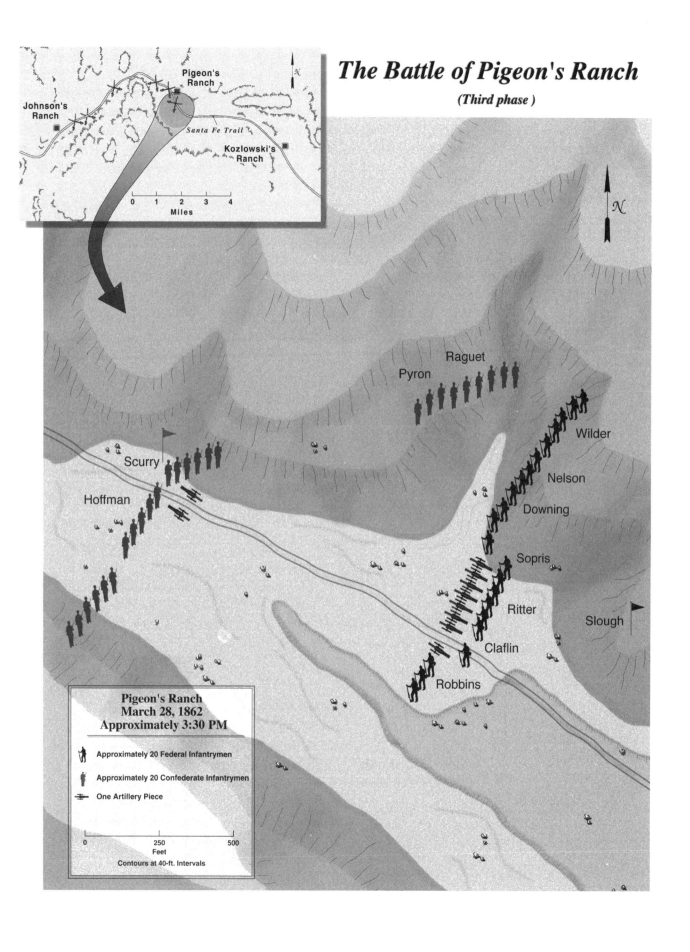

The Battle of Pigeon's Ranch
(Third phase)

Johnson's Ranch

Pigeon's Ranch

Santa Fe Trail

Kozlowski's Ranch

0 1 2 3 4
Miles

N

Pyron

Raguet

Wilder

Nelson

Downing

Sopris

Scurry

Hoffman

Ritter

Slough

Claflin

Robbins

**Pigeon's Ranch
March 28, 1862
Approximately 3:30 PM**

Approximately 20 Federal Infantrymen

Approximately 20 Confederate Infantrymen

One Artillery Piece

0   250   500
Feet
Contours at 40-ft. Intervals

to move the wagons to what he considered a safe location. Instead the train was parked less than a mile east of Pigeon's Ranch, where it remained until Slough finally gave the order to withdraw shortly after 4:00 P.M. By then the situation was critical. The infantry was falling back and not all of the wagons were yet in motion. When the combatants finally did stop and establish a new position, it was beyond the area where the wagons had been parked. Advancing Texans fired several shots at the trailing wagons as the train rumbled down the road toward Kozlowski's. All but two wagons escaped and those were set afire to make sure their contents were of no use to the Texans.[22]

Though he had few alternatives, Captain Gurden Chapin, serving as Slough's adjutant, selected an ideal location for the final artillery position. About three-quarters of a mile east of the ranch, just north of the Santa Fe Trail and beyond a large open space, the site offered good cover for the supports as well as an open field of fire for the cannon. Again Ritter was on the right and Claflin on the left.[23]

The Confederates were tired but they had momentum now; and they still had their minds set on capturing some Yankee artillery pieces as trophies of the battle, just as they had at Valverde. Major Henry Raguet was pushing forward on the extreme left. As recounted by his brother-in-law, Frank Starr, a private in the Fourth Texas:

> Henry took a party of the men to drive them from the rocks. The enemy's fire was so terrible that our boys faltered. Henry rushed on, cheering the boys to follow him. He took a direction around the left of the rocks, calling the boys on, saying that we could get around them and cut off their retreat. All this time Henry was within 20 steps of the rocks and his uniform, words, and actions attracting the attention of the enemy—many of them were shooting at him with their pistols but until that moment he had escaped with a ball through his coat sleeves. But then he fell—a ball passing through his body. . . . Henry lived about one hour and a half—Captain Foard from Angelina was with him from the time he fell until he expired.[24]

This tragedy for the Texans had its counterpart on the Colorado side. According to Whitford, the young private who shot Raguet had had a premonition the night before and had told Captain Downing, "I dreamed last night that I was shot through my heart in battle today." Downing downplayed the dream; but sure enough, a Texas sharpshooter fired back at the muzzle flash of the round that killed Raguet. The bullet hit the young man's rifle and ricocheted into his chest, piercing his heart. His last words were, "I told you something would happen!"[25]

In the meantime Raguet's boys continued to engage the Coloradans in the rocks in what was said to be one of the most terrible fights of the day. Then there was a lull, and with most of the wagons at a safe distance down the road, the Federal cannon were limbered and the drivers told to follow the train. The Federal infantry fell in behind the artillery; the Texans stayed put; and the Battle of Pigeon's Ranch was over.[26]

This time it had been the Federals who were "outflanked and outgeneraled." Slough got off to a bad start when he tried to double flank the Texans, sending a single company to each side, while holding more than a third of his force in reserve. Captain Downing, who led the attack on the left, considered it a miracle that anyone escaped the "ambush into which the God of War had sent Company D."[27]

And despite almost constantly giving ground, Colonel Slough never engaged his regular cavalry.[28] Private Hollister, a member of Company F, the Colorado cavalry, wrote:

> The regular cavalry was no account at all, for whenever the Texans came in sight they would mount and fall back out of range. Walker's company never discharged a single rifle during the day.[29]

It may have been that Slough had finally begun to take Colonel Canby's orders to heart, remembering that he had been advised to hold the regular cavalry in reserve.[30] Or there may have been some truth to the recollections of Slough's aide, James Farmer, who at age eighty-one, wrote that the colonel had sent him after the cavalry with an order to charge the Texans, but Captain Lord did not carry out the instructions, a failure for which he was much "censored" by the officers.[31]

It seems more likely that the failure was Slough's, and one must wonder if the hundred or so men of the First and Third U.S. Cavalry (dismounted) might have made a critical difference on the rocky ridge that overlooked Pigeon's Ranch.[32]

8

Disaster at Johnson's Ranch

THE SUN HAD ALREADY CLEARED THE HILLS TO THE EAST ON THE morning of March 28 when Major Chivington and his battalion left Kozlowski's Ranch, some thirty minutes ahead of the rest of Slough's command.[1] This part of the Federal force had been given a special assignment, one that would prove critical to the day's results. In fact Union apologist Ovando Hollister would later describe it as "striking a blow which pierced to the [Confederate] vitals and drew from them the life's blood."[2]

By the evening of March 27, Slough and Chivington knew that Pyron had been reinforced by Scurry and the Fourth Texas. Armed with this knowledge, they had decided to risk splitting their force to strike simultaneously at the Confederate's front and rear. Slough felt that the Texans would remain at Johnson's Ranch, so he decided to conduct a two-pronged attack (a move he would later refer to as a reconnaissance-in-force). He would march down the canyon on the Santa Fe Trail, while Chivington would swing well south of the main trail, climb and cross Glorieta Mesa, and hit the Texan rear while Slough engaged their front.[3] If this maneuver could be properly coordinated, the Union forces would surely emerge victorious.

With Chivington on the morning of March 28 were about 530 officers and men who had been divided into three groups: two infantry columns, roughly equal in size, plus a detachment from Company K of the Third U.S. Cavalry.[4] One of the columns was led by Captain William Lewis of the Fifth U.S. Infantry, assisted by Captain A. B. Carey (Seventh U.S. Infantry). Lewis's column included companies A and G of the Fifth U.S. Infantry under Lieutenants Samuel Barr and Stephen Norvell, Company B of the First Colorado under forty-year-old Leadville miner and blacksmith Captain Samuel Logan, and a mixed company of Fourth New

Mexico Volunteers and miscellaneous Coloradans under the command of Captain James Ford and Lieutenant Cyrus DeForrest.[5]

The second column was led by Captain Edward Wynkoop and consisted of three companies of the First Colorado: Company A under Lieutenant James Shaffer, Company E under Captain Scott Anthony, and Company H under Captain George Sanborn and Lieutenant Byron Sanford. At the request of Colonel Slough, Chivington was also accompanied by Colonel James Collins, a prominent New Mexico newspaperman, Valverde veteran, and the current Indian Agent in Santa Fe.[6] The men were said to be "full of jubilant enthusiasm" such that it was "only necessary for Chivington to lead for them to conquer."[7]

One mile northwest of Kozlowski's ranch, the battalion passed the long-abandoned ruins of the old Pecos Pueblo and, after following Glorieta Creek for another three miles, turned west-southwest along the road to Galisteo, which soon turned south through San Cristobal Canyon.[8] Chivington's battalion was guided on its special mission by Lieutenant Colonel Manuel Chaves, a forty-four-year-old officer in the Second New Mexico Volunteers. Chaves was a veteran of the Mexican War and the Taos Rebellion, a former Santa Fe Trail merchant, a well-known New Mexico Indian fighter, and most recently, a veteran of the Battle of Valverde.[9]

The Galisteo road climbed with a slight grade for the first two miles, then steepened sharply for a short distance until the command found itself on the rolling terrain atop Glorieta Mesa. After riding about a mile further south, Chaves indicated that the battalion should turn onto a faint trail which led westward off the main road.[10]

Chivington and Slough knew (or suspected) that before the action in Apache Canyon on the twenty-sixth, Scurry and the Fourth Texas had been encamped at or near the village of Galisteo, twenty miles or so to the south. They also knew that somewhere to the south were Sibley, Green, and the rest of the Confederate army. Therefore the Coloradans were more than a little concerned about being cut off from the rest of the Federal force should more Texans come to the fight along the Galisteo road. Irish-born Lieutenant John Falvey and the forty troopers from Company K of the Third U.S. Cavalry were detailed to scout south on the Galisteo road to provide some advance warning should this threat materialize.[11]

The Coloradans parted company with Falvey's cavalry around

Captain Samuel Logan,
First Colorado Volun-
teers (courtesy Colo-
rado Historical Society)

midmorning and turned west, paralleling the main canyon. Shortly thereafter, they may have heard the first deep rumblings of cannon fire from Pigeon's Ranch. Given everyone's prior expectation that the fight would occur further west at Johnson's Ranch and given the role that simultaneity played in Slough's strategy, this would have furrowed the brow of the big Colorado preacher; but not knowing just where the cannon fire came from or what it meant, he could only press forward and pray fervently that Slough's plan would still succeed.[12]

The top of Glorieta Mesa was (and still is) a rolling countryside covered with pine trees and scrub cedar. Chaves, who had scouted these heights with Manuel Armijo to oppose Kearny's advance during the Mexican War and who had traveled the area extensively, knew a relatively easy route to the northwestern edge of the mesa, and he led the command along this trail. Reaching the western escarpment between 1:30 and 2:00 in the afternoon, Chaves pointed down to Johnson's Ranch, seven hundred feet below, and said to Chivington, "You are right on top of them, Major."[13]

Scurry had stationed a single sentry on top of the Mesa but, asleep at his post, he was captured before he could sound a warning to those below.[14] Telling his company commanders to keep the men quiet and out of sight, Chivington moved to the edge of the cliff and surveyed the scene before him. From his aerie perch, the Union commander looked down on the entire Confederate supply train, neatly arrayed in and around the ranch. There looked to be about two hundred Texans, between sixty and seventy wagons, several hundred horses and mules, and a field hospital. Shifting his gaze to the terrain itself, he could see that the northwest face of Glorieta Mesa was a steep precipice with scrub-covered talus slopes. The first three hundred feet or so below his location dropped off sharply then the slope lessened enough to allow men to climb down unaided. The slope ended adjacent to Galisteo Creek, several hundred yards south of Johnson's Ranch. The Texans had set up a lone six-pounder on the highest of several knolls that commanded the western end of Apache Canyon, across a small arroyo from the ranch. The bulk of the men appeared to be leisurely encamped, completely oblivious to the threat above them on the mesa.[15]

Despite the fact that he had apparently achieved total surprise, Chivington was not entirely comfortable with his situation. First of all there was no sign of the main Confederate force. Second there was no

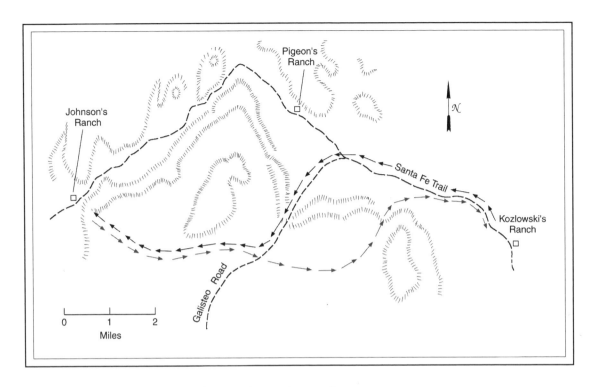

Chivington's Route to and from Johnson's Ranch
(Graphics by David Cunnington)

sign of Slough. Could this be a trap? Chivington reviewed his options. He and his men were in a totally indefensible position at the edge of a cliff. The Confederate force below him appeared to be small and disorganized enough for his Coloradans to easily overwhelm it, but between him and the Rebels was the seven-hundred-foot precipice—once his men started down, they would be committed. If Scurry was lurking nearby or if Green or Sibley was on the march from Santa Fe or Galisteo, Chivington could find himself in a real bind. On the other hand, the unanticipated opportunity to destroy the Texans' supplies could not be ignored. In addition, the 260-pound major must have realized that while he personally could probably get down the cliff, getting back up might well be impossible.

Between 2:00 and 3:00 P.M. Chivington finally decided that the supply train was too attractive a target and that he had to take the risk.[16] He ordered the battalion to descend to the base of the mesa and attack the camp. Ropes and straps, probably including some saddle leathers and spare halters, were required near the top and dislodged rocks and brush began to tumble down the canyon walls, alerting the Texans who rushed up the knoll to the cannon and began firing. But the volleys slammed ineffectually into the hillside and the Federals were able to reach the bottom of the mesa unscathed and set up a line of battle in about thirty minutes.[17] Chivington and a small picket force remained at the top of the bluff, while command of the attack was detailed to Captain Lewis.[18]

After a quick check of the area, the Federals confirmed that they were opposed by a small, disorganized force and only the single piece of artillery. Immediately Captain Lewis, Lieutenant Sanford, and the rest of Company H of the First Colorado moved toward the knoll east of the ranch in an effort to capture the cannon. The remainder of the battalion, probably led by Captain Wynkoop, swept onto Johnson's Ranch.

The Confederate camp was guarded by a hodgepodge of sick and injured soldiers, cooks, teamsters, plus the few artillerymen from the Fifth Texas led by Private Timothy Nettles, a twenty-four-year-old telegraph contractor originally from Darlington, South Carolina.[19] The senior officer appears to have been thirty-two-year-old Second Lieutenant John Taylor of Company I of the Fifth Texas. When this disorganized olio was faced with two columns of onrushing Federal troops, most of the men quickly broke and ran. Although Nettles and others of the Fifth Texas manned the cannon atop the knoll, many leapt aboard horses and mules and rode west toward Santa Fe. Others fled up the Santa Fe Trail toward Pigeon's Ranch, some on foot and some on horseback. A few brave souls tried to defend the wagons, but they quickly realized their cause was futile. The picture on the Confederate side was one of complete chaos.

Private Nettles saw that the loss of the cannon was inevitable, so he abandoned the piece and ran back and torched off the limber box which exploded, injuring him slightly. Lewis, Sanford, and some of the men of the First Colorado reached the cannon after it was abandoned, spiked the piece with a ramrod and a six-pounder ball, and rolled it down the hillside.[20]

Within a few minutes it was all over. The Federals had suffered only one man killed and six wounded, one mortally. The Texans had lost two killed, two wounded, and seventeen captured.[21] But more important, the critical supply train was in Union hands.

Ever more nervous about their precarious situation, the Pike's Peakers were ordered to line up the prisoners and "shoot them" if the main body of Texans appeared. Taking umbrage at this affront to chivalry, William Davidson of Company A of the Fifth Texas, later described Chivington's men as

> a set of miscreants. They are certainly no part or parcel of the brave men we have been confronting and fighting for the last six weeks. The men who have been fighting us would scorn to do what they did and would scorn them for doing it. They fired on our hospital of sick and wounded men and when Parson Jones [Episcopal Pastor Lucius Jones, the chaplain of the Fourth Texas] saw that they would not respect a yellow flag, he took a white flag and went out in front of the hospital and stood and waved it until they came up and shot him down.[22]

Scurry also suggested that the Federals "had lost all sense of humanity," something that Major Chivington would be accused of again a few years later at Sand Creek, Colorado.[23] These sentiments were echoed by Harvey Holcomb of Company F of the Fourth Texas who called Chivington a "contemptible coward" for ordering sick and wounded Confederates to be "shot down like dogs" if the main body of the Texans appeared.[24]

The afternoon shadows were beginning to lengthen and all of the concerns that had worried the Coloradans when they arrived at the overlook still remained. Where was Scurry? Where was Slough? What about the persistent rumors of heavy reinforcements marching north from Galisteo?[25] Liberated Union prisoners, captured during the fight at Pigeon's Ranch, told Lewis and his men about the early afternoon retreat of Slough in the face of Scurry's persistent Texans, saying "they had killed nearly all of us and had driven the balance from the canon [sic]."[26] Thus there was a major uncertainty about what dangers awaited if, as originally planned, Chivington moved up the Santa Fe Trail to threaten Scurry's rear.

When the intelligence from the prisoners was relayed to Chivington on the top of the mesa, he decided that to follow the standing orders to attack the Texan rear would be too risky and that the battalion should return to the Union lines by way of the mesa route. Although this was an apparent violation of orders, it was probably a fortuitous decision. By

Painting of the Union Raid on Johnson's Ranch by N. Eggenhofer (courtesy Fort Union National Monument)

the time the Confederate detachment at Johnson's Ranch had been subdued and the Federal forces were reassembled, it was nearly sundown and the Coloradans were still two or three hours away from Pigeon's Ranch. By the time Chivington reached Pigeon's, Scurry would no longer have had Slough to worry about and the nighttime engagement between the two exhausted forces would have been an interesting one with an uncertain outcome. Nonetheless, at the same time Chivington was making his difficult decision, both Slough and Tappan were still anticipating the arrival of his troops to aid their deteriorating situation at Pigeon's Ranch. Lieutenant Colonel Tappan later wrote that it was the possibility of Chivington's arrival that caused him to hold his fire on one occasion and that earlier in the afternoon this is what Slough "expected at every moment."

The decision not to march back to Pigeon's along the canyon route meant that the soldiers would have to climb back up the steep mesa wall, so it was clearly not possible to take the supplies and animals. Therefore the decision was made to destroy the train. Under the direction of Captain Lewis, the men grouped the wagons together, turned several of them over, and set the contents on fire.[27] Private Simon Ritter, Company A of the First Colorado, was severely injured when one of the ammunition wagons exploded with unexpected force.

Most of the mules were probably driven off down the canyon. However there are persistent stories of a massive slaughter of the mules by the Coloradans. In his memoirs, Chivington said that they bayoneted eleven hundred animals.[28] Gardiner says that three hundred were killed, and the anonymous author of *The March of the First* says that the Pike's Peakers shot all but fourteen of the animals.[29] Oliva points out that bayoneting or shooting several hundred animals would have been a dangerous, time-consuming endeavor; and H. C. Wright, writing some sixty-five years later, said, "We did not have over 500 [mules] and I for one never saw or heard of a dead one."[30] However, near-real-time reports by participants should not be totally discounted, so it seems probable that some animals were intentionally dispatched by Chivington's men.

Reassembling near the base of the mesa, the Federals and their prisoners began the arduous seven-hundred-foot ascent. Part way up an alert observer noted that four wagons had been overlooked behind a bluff back at Johnson's Ranch. Not wishing to leave Scurry with any supplies at all, four volunteers clambered back down and set the last wagons ablaze, returning to the rest of the force at the top of the Mesa within an hour.[31]

Shortly after Chivington's command had reassembled at the top of the mesa, they were met by a messenger, dispatched by Colonel Slough in the early afternoon, who reported that Slough had been "driven from his position with considerable loss" and that he requested "immediate aid." Chivington himself noted that he was directed to "advance to support the main column," an order which he "hastened to obey."[32]

Responding to Slough's urgent request, Chivington's men quickly began to retrace their steps in the failing daylight.[33] They had marched about five miles, reaching the area near the Galisteo road, when Slough's aide-de-camp, Lieutenant Alfred Cobb of Company C of the First Colorado, intercepted the column. Cobb had been dispatched from the fight at Pigeon's Ranch by the beleaguered colonel after the final retreat in the late afternoon.[34] According to Chivington, Cobb countermanded the first messenger's directives, noting that "we were ruined and that retreat had been ordered to Koslosky's [sic]."[35]

Cobb further reported that if Chivington did not change his route and "proceed by some by-way he would surely be cut off." Receipt of this information put the Union forces in another dilemma—Chaves was most familiar with the route the battalion had taken in the morning but, in light of Cobb's report, that route could very likely lead the Coloradans right into Texan-controlled territory. By now it was completely dark, so attempting to blaze a new trail across the mesa appeared to be an equally unattractive option.

Suddenly, out of the gloom rode a large man on a white horse. He and Chaves were soon engaged in an animated conversation in Spanish. After a moment or two, Chaves broke off the conversation and introduced Chivington to the local priest-turned-businessman, Alexander Grzelachowski. Affectionately known as "Padre Polaco," the thirty-eight-year-old native of Poland had left the priesthood in 1857 after serving the Catholic church for nine years, most recently at the Parish of Our Lady of Sorrows in Manzano, New Mexico. After leaving Manzano and the priesthood, Grzelachowski had moved to Las Vegas, New Mexico, and opened a business, so he was very familiar with La Glorieta Pass. Padre Polaco had also volunteered as the chaplain of the Second New Mexico Volunteers, and consequently he was well acquainted with Lieutenant Colonel Chaves.[36]

Grzelachowski confirmed that returning to Kozlowski's Ranch by way of the Galisteo Road would be risky indeed, but he offered to lead Chivington's command along an alternative route with which he was familiar and which he said would avoid the Texan invaders and return the Union troops safely to Kozlowski's. Although he must have had second thoughts, Chivington felt that he had no choice, so the decision was made and Grzelachowski led off on horseback followed by Chivington and the rest of the battalion. Crossing the Galisteo road, some of the men must have looked longingly north toward Pigeon's Ranch as they left the cleared, flat roadway and climbed once again into the gloom of the mountainous scrub and pine forest.

In order to avoid enemy territory, Grzelachowski led the force south of their morning's route. From the Galisteo road, they proceeded east–southeast to the edge of the mesa, probably near the point where one of

Lieutenant Colonel Manuel Chaves, Second New Mexico Volunteers (courtesy New Mexico Photo Archives, neg.#9833)

the tributaries of Padre Springs Creek runs down from the top of the mesa. There, in the late evening, the battalion descended the steep escarpment about three and one-half miles west of Kozlowski's Ranch.[37] The terrain the battalion followed during the night was much rougher than that traversed during their morning march, so rough in fact, that part way back, Grzelachowski's big white horse dropped dead from exhaustion,[38] and one of the infantrymen exclaimed:

> Deep ravines and rough mountains, each alternately formed the base line of our pedestrian journey throughout that hitherto unfrequented track on a dark night, rendered still more gloomy by the heavy tall trees which grew all along our way. I can safely say that not one half mile of fair level ground was at any time traveled during the 15 miles of ups and downs back to camp, added to which we suffered from a violent thirst, no water being had since morning.[39]

Alexander
Grzelachowski
(courtesy Francis
Kajenki)

Sometime between 10:00 P.M. on the twenty-eighth and the wee hours of the twenty-ninth, Chivington's men found themselves near enough to Kozlowski's Ranch to see campfires and hear the subdued voices of soldiers. But whose fires and voices were they? The ever-optimistic Chivington later recalled saying, "It doesn't matter—if they're rebels, we will take them and if our fellows, we will join them."[40] Then, taking no chances, the battalion formed a line of battle, fixed bayonets, and approached the flickering lights. As the exhausted men neared the encampment, a sentry called out a challenge—it was a Yankee voice! Finally the battalion was in friendly territory—the men marched into camp and stacked their arms.

9

Aftermath

THE CLIMACTIC FIGHT AT PIGEON'S RANCH HAD SLOWLY GROUND TO A halt as the Texans watched the Union infantrymen disappear down the Santa Fe Trail in the failing afternoon light. Scurry evaluated his situation—there was nothing to be gained and much to be put at risk if he ordered his exhausted charges to pursue the retreating Federals, and he was on a battlefield littered with the detritus of a major fight. Dead and wounded men and animals covered the ranch complex, and cries and moans could be heard from one edge of the valley to the other.

There really was no choice—Scurry had to formally stop the fighting so that both sides could tend to their casualties. Turning to an aide, he asked for something white that could be used to cross the battle lines. When nothing was forthcoming, the colonel bellowed, "God damn it, tear off your shirt tail, we have got to have a white flag!" Private Harvey Holcomb, standing nearby had just picked up a white silk handkerchief. He later recalled:

> I hated to give it up, but after looking around I decided there was not
> a shirt tail in the crowd that would do for a white flag, they would have
> suited better for battle flags, so I walked up and gave the colonel my
> much prized silk handkerchief. He said it was just the thing.[1]

Handing the handkerchief to Major Alexander Jackson,[2] Scurry directed that a truce be requested to bury the dead and care for the wounded. Jackson immediately climbed into a nearby ambulance and headed east toward the retreating Federals. Down the trail a mile or so, he crossed the rear of the Union lines commanded by Captain Downing. Blindfolding the Texan so as not to reveal their true state of disarray, the Coloradans escorted him to Colonel Slough, who by now was back at Kozlowski's Ranch. Slough agreed to a thirty-six hour truce.[3]

There has been considerable debate over the years as to Scurry's motivation for "calling off the dogs" in light of his clear victory on the field of battle. In his report, he said that he stopped and did not pursue only because his men were exhausted. Others have argued that he was demoralized because he had found out about Chivington's success at Johnson's Ranch. It is entirely possible that Scurry had heard about the attack on Johnson's Ranch by 4:00 P.M., but not likely that he had details on the extent of the destruction. In fact it may be that Peticolas was correct when he wrote that Scurry did not learn of the loss of the supply train until noon on the following day.

Regardless of Scurry's rationale for stopping the fight and requesting a truce, it meant that there was work to do; and almost as soon as the tired men of the First Colorado had stacked their arms at Kozlowski's Ranch, they were climbing into wagons to return to the battlefield. This was the "other side" of battle—the search for dead and wounded comrades. As they reached Pigeon's Ranch, the men fanned out across the canyon in the fading daylight, shovels and stretchers in hand, tending to their grim task as the snow once again began to fall.[4]

The Coloradans traversed the wooded hillsides, mingling with their Texan counterparts, no doubt warily at first, but soon almost oblivious to allegiance, the moans of the wounded and the stark reality of the mangled dead transcending the political differences that had divided them only hours before.[5]

Because the Texan supplies, or what remained of them, were six miles to the rear at Johnson's Ranch, Scurry's men had none of the tools needed to perform their dreary work. So the Texans asked the Coloradans for shovels and a peculiar form of cooperation took place among these erstwhile enemies.[6]

Private B. H. Tyler of Company F of the Fourth Texas recalled:

> We went about gathering up our dead and putting them away which we did as best we could. We dug a big hole large enough for them and laid them two deep and spread a layer of blankets over them and filled in on them with dirt. It was bad but the best we could do.[7]

The battle in and around Pigeon's Ranch had raged for over five hours. Heavy fighting had occurred flank-to-flank as the lines moved more than a mile down the wooded valley, so there were wounded men and bodies scattered over a large area. Scurry had lost 111 men: 42 killed, 61 wounded, and 14 prisoners (six of the latter among the wounded). As the preliminary casualty list came in, the colonel must have felt a shiver, for it cut right through the cream of his officer corps—Henry Raguet, "Shrop" Shropshire, Isaac Adair, and Charles Buckholts all dead. In addition, James Bradford, his sole artillery commander, was wounded; and Denman Shannon had been captured.[8]

Even Pyron, the only one of the three majors to survive the fight, had a close call when his horse was killed under him. According to one account, the horse was "shot in two by a cannon ball."[9] Scurry himself knew about the intensity of the fighting firsthand—he had had several near misses: his cheek had been grazed and there were bullet holes in his grimy uniform.[10]

These setbacks notwithstanding, the Confederate commander painted a glorious picture in his General Order to the troops dated March 29:

> Soldiers—You have added another victory to the long list of triumphs won by the Confederate armies. By your conduct, you have given another evidence of the daring courage and heroic endurance which actuate you in this great struggle for the independence of your country. You have proven your right to stand by the side of those who fought and conquered on the red field of San Jacinto. The battle of Glorietta [sic]—where for six long hours you steadily drove before you a foe of twice your numbers—over a field chosen by themselves and deemed impregnable, will take its place upon the rolls of your country's triumphs, and serve to excite your children to imitate the brave deeds of their fathers, in every hour of that country's peril.
>
> Soldiers—I am proud of you. Go on as you have commenced and it will not be long until not a single soldier of the United States will be left upon the soil of New Mexico. The Territory, relieved of the burden imposed on it by its late oppressors, will once more, throughout its beautiful valleys, "blossom as the rose," beneath the plastic hand of peaceful industry.[11]

Thomas Ochiltree, Sibley's assistant adjutant general; a Marshall, Texas lawyer; Jefferson, Texas newspaperman; and glib-tongued future Texas governor, was even more hyperbolic in an April 27 dispatch to President Jefferson Davis:

I have the honor to inform your Excellency of another glorious victory achieved by the Confederate Army of New Mexico. . . . Texas volunteers met, attacked, whipped, and routed 2,000 Federals, 23 miles
east of Santa Fe. . . . The enemy's loss was over seven hundred killed
and wounded—five hundred being left on the field. Their rout was
complete and they were scattered from the battlefield to Fort Union.[12]

The truth was that Slough had suffered 138 casualties at Pigeon's
Ranch—47 killed, 78 wounded, 11 prisoners, and 2 deserters—nothing
like the numbers reported by Ochiltree, but more than he had inflicted
on Scurry and certainly a bloody baptism of fire for his previously untested Pike's Peakers. So the evening campfire chatter at Kozlowski's
Ranch was much more subdued on the night of the twenty-eighth than
on the previous night, for each man could look around him and see that
comrades who had shared breakfast here on the morning of the cold
spring day had not returned at day's end. This mood may have improved
slightly when Chivington and his men arrived with word of their success at Johnson's Ranch.

Slough's impetuous "reconnaissance-in-force" had cost him about
10 percent casualties, and a capable opponent still controlled the Santa
Fe Trail just a few miles to the west. The Coloradan could not be sure of
Scurry's next move. Would he wait for reinforcements from Albuquerque and Santa Fe and then pounce on the debilitated Coloradans, or
would he fall back to the capital and regroup before striking east again?
Given these uncertainties, the Colorado commander felt uncomfortable
staying at Kozlowski's Ranch for a protracted period of time.

On March 29, Slough ordered the command to fall back to Bernal
Springs; and by 2:00 P.M. they had evacuated all but the most gravely
wounded soldiers from the makeshift field hospital and were once again
on the road. Napoleon Kozlowski later reported,

When they camped on my place and while they made my tavern their
hospital for over two months after their battles in the canyon, they
never robbed me of anything, not even a chicken.[13]

Apparently the Coloradans had learned their lessons about foraging.

Slough reported to the adjutant general that "the enemy in a mountain canyon are too strong to make battle with my force" so he would
"now occupy a position to protect Fort Union and, at the same time,
harass and damage the enemy."[14]

By the twenty-ninth, Scurry realized that he was in no condition to pursue Slough. His men were tired and hungry, and Chivington had seen to it that he had no food, ammunition, or blankets close at hand. The Texans had suffered 16 percent casualties and needed to regroup. With all this in mind, early on the morning of the twenty-ninth Scurry sent another aide to Slough to request an extension of the truce until 8:00 A.M. on the thirtieth to deal with the dead and wounded.[15]

Despite the appearances and the feelings of some of the men, "Dirty Shirt" Scurry was not ready to let Slough off the hook. In his report to Sibley he asked for ammunition and declared, "as soon as I am fixed for it, I wish to get after them again."[16]

Scurry may have underestimated the impact felt by his "unfed and blanketless" troops. Davidson, for example, said,

> Here we are between two armies, one double ours and the other four times our number, 1,000 miles from home, not a wagon, not a dust of flour, not a pound of meat. . . . nothing to eat, but we had breakfast this morning and we'll feast on the recollection of that![17]

Harvey Holcomb said,

> If the Union commander had only known our condition and held out until 12 o'clock the next day, the Confederates would have had to surrender as we had no rations and our ammunition was about exhausted.[18]

So late on the twenty-ninth, Scurry's command headed out of Glorieta Pass, past Apache Canyon, toward Santa Fe, twenty-two miles to the west. Marching all night, the column began straggling into Santa Fe on the thirtieth and continued to come in by twos and threes all day.

Louisa Hawkins Canby, wife of the Union commander, and several other Union officer's wives had remained in Santa Fe during the Confederate incursion. Mrs. Canby had suspected that there might be a major fight and so she and the other wives were prepared to assist with injured men. When wounded soldiers began to arrive, it made no difference that they were Confederates—Mrs. Canby and the other women nursed the men in their own homes "like they were her own sons," ignoring the differences that had brought them here in the first place.[19]

The care by the Union wives was greatly appreciated by the sick and wounded Texans, so much so that on May 31, 1862, a group of Confederates published a resolution in the *Santa Fe Gazette*:

> Resolved that we should be doing violence to our feelings were we to leave this place without expressing to the ladies of Santa Fe and, through them, to those who have aided them in their mission, our proformed [sic] gratitude for the delicate kindness which has been shown to many of us in suffering and sickness and the attention and courtesy which has been extended by all.[20]

Colonel Slough's actions following the Battle of Glorieta Pass are also fraught with questions. One of course is why he continued to retreat. With the return of Chivington's command, he outnumbered Scurry—now badly crippled for want of supplies—by a healthy margin, perhaps two to one. The answer, according to Slough's report to the adjutant general, was that "the enemy in a mountain canyon are too strong to make battle with my force." That being the case, Slough went on to say that he would "now occupy a position to protect Fort Union and at the same time harass and damage the enemy."[21] The first part of the statement does not seem to hold water; the second part is clearly a reference to Canby's orders, but whether reflecting honest obedience or an excuse to avoid further conflict is another question.

In camp at Bernal Springs on the thirty-first, Slough received orders from Colonel Canby to fall back all the way to Fort Union. According to Private Hollister,

> to obey [the order] was to let the enemy. . . . escape; to refuse was to subject himself to court-martial and disgrace. He issued the order for backward movement, but resigned his commission.[22]

Slough seemed to be telling his men one thing and Washington another. Certainly by falling back to Bernal Springs on the twenty-ninth he was not inhibiting a Confederate retreat! It would appear that the obstreperous Colorado colonel was looking for an excuse for resignation. He was obviously worried that Colonel Paul had been right all along and that he might well be in for a court-martial for violation of Canby's orders of March 16 and 18. Moreover there was no assurance that obedience to the orders just received would restore him to the good graces of the department commander.

And there was yet another problem. Slough had been unpopular with his troops from the beginning, but his performance in the previous day's battle caused his stock to reach a new low. His actions seemed cowardly to those who noticed that he had spent most of the day well to the rear of the action and had sent Captain Chapin forward whenever it was necessary to communicate with those near the front. In fact Slough was told by one of his officers that he [Slough] had been deliberately fired upon by his own men![23]

According to Colonel Slough himself, the reason for his resignation was fear for his personal safety. In a letter Slough wrote to Sam Tappan almost a year later Slough stated,

> at the battle of Pigeon's Ranch a volley was fired at me . . . hence I hid myself from that flank so as to avoid a repetition—this is what gave rise to the report that I acted cowardly at the time—I resigned the colonelcy because I was satisfied that a further connection would result in my assassination. I am now satisfied that men now in high rank and command were at the bottom of this thing. I am satisfied that today if a chance offered I would be murdered.[24]

Little did the good colonel know what Fate held for him but a few years later in a Santa Fe barroom!

And so it may have been for a combination of reasons that Slough submitted his resignation, effective April 9, and returned command of the northern wing of Canby's army to the sulking Colonel Paul.

Slough's resignation presented several opportunities for promotion within the First Colorado Volunteers. Logically the colonelcy would devolve to the lieutenant colonel, but Tappan felt obliged to step aside in favor of Major Chivington, the popular hero of Apache Canyon and Johnson's Ranch. Clearly this stuck in Tappan's craw because from that point on he was an avowed opponent of the "Fighting Parson," so much so that in January 1863 he wrote to Chivington:

> From the earliest organization of our regiment you have done your utmost by outspoken remarks and secret intimation to destroy my influence as an officer in the regiment.[25]

It took a day and a night for the news from Glorieta Pass to reach Confederate Army headquarters in Albuquerque. Private William Henry Smith wrote in his journal on March 30:

We this morning received the most glorious news from Santa Fe. Col. Scurry with the first [sic] regiment whipped five regiments of Kansas soldiers, whipped the Kansas fellows greatly.[26]

Sibley's band struck up Dixie and the Rebel cheers rang through the streets of Albuquerque. The soldiers no doubt had less than the whole story, but even if they knew about the destruction of Scurry's train, that would not have been as important to these Texans as winning the fight.[27]

Colonel Scurry's written report to General Sibley at headquarters in Albuquerque was not so jubilant. He stated that the loss of his supplies so crippled him that he was unable to follow up the victory and was compelled to go to Santa Fe for "something to eat." Then, expressing optimism regarding the prospects for resupply, Scurry went on to say that as soon as he was fixed for it, he wished to "get after them again."[28]

Sibley apparently took Scurry's report at face value. There still being no sign of a northward move by Canby, the general dispatched the remainder of the Fifth Regiment under Colonel Green to Santa Fe to reinforce operations against Slough. Sibley would follow and take command of the renewed offensive. The four companies guarding the depots at Cubero and Albuquerque could safely remain behind, inasmuch as Canby, when he did move, would surely take a route east of the mountains to join Slough at or near Fort Union.

Before departing Albuquerque, General Sibley wrote two letters, one to the adjutant general in Richmond and the other to the governor of Texas. He began the message to General Cooper on a positive note, "I have the honor and pleasure to report another victory," but he concluded both letters with an identical and almost desperate plea, "I must have reinforcements. . . . Send me reinforcements."[29] Sibley recognized the increased possibility of being faced by the combined forces of Canby and Slough; but for now, he would take the initiative and hit Slough again before Canby moved north.[30]

At 3:00 in the afternoon of March 30 Colonel Green's six companies departed Albuquerque for Santa Fe, followed the next day by Sibley and his headquarters staff.[31] Upon his arrival in Santa Fe on April 5, the Confederate general found:

> the whole exultant army assembled. The sick and wounded had been comfortably quartered and attended; the loss of clothing and trans-

portation had been made up from the enemy's stores and confisca-
tions; and, indeed, everything done which should have been done.[32]

Sanguine as he was upon his arrival at Santa Fe, Sibley began to have
second thoughts about an offensive against Fort Union. The troops may
have been comfortable for the moment, but food and forage were still in
short supply. Despite the discovery of a cache of blankets and other supplies that James Collins had attempted to hide behind a plastered-up
doorway at the Indian Agency headquarters, Santa Fe was by now pretty
well used up.[33] The Confederates were really in no better position to as-
sault Fort Union than they had been a month and a half earlier to deal
with Fort Craig. Slough could easily hold the fort until Canby arrived,
and then the Confederates would be heavily outnumbered and at a serious disadvantage.

One alternative was to move south to a location where reinforcements and supplies might be secured from Texas or, failing that, a retreat
could be effected from New Mexico. After much discussion, the plan
agreed upon was to move Sibley's entire command to the village of
Manzano (Padre Polaco's old haunt), some sixty miles southeast of Albuquerque, securing as a line of communication the road to Mesilla, via
Fort Stanton. Even before this plan was put into motion, however, it was,
as General Sibley put it, "disconcerted" by the news that Federal forces
from Fort Craig were advancing on Albuquerque.[34]

Colonel Canby had departed Fort Craig on April 1, the day after he received a message from Slough reporting the engagement at Apache Canyon. The obvious route to a junction with Slough was by way of Abo
Pass (just south of Manzano) to the east side of the mountains, then
northwest toward Fort Union. But realizing that this was what Sibley
expected, Canby decided to march up the Rio Grande to Albuquerque
and cross the mountains through Carnuel Pass. He would take Albuquerque, if it could be done without serious loss, or at least by making a
demonstration against the town, he would draw the main Confederate
force down from Santa Fe, thereby facilitating the junction with Slough.[35]

When he arrived within range of Albuquerque on the afternoon of
April 8, Canby unlimbered his artillery and opened fire. The Confederates responded with their own cannon, moving each of the three pieces

among several locations to create the illusion of greater strength. The cannonading and skirmishing continued for a day and a half; then the Federal commander employed a bit of deception (probably unnecessary in light of his overwhelmingly superior numbers) and brought the affair to an end. On the night of April 9, Canby's troops lit their campfires, the bugler called tattoo, and the Federal force stole away through Tijeras Canyon under cover of darkness.[36]

One can only speculate whether Sibley was disappointed or relieved that Canby had called off the attack and slipped through the pass before the arrival of the main Confederate force. In any case, there was now little prospect for holding out at Manzano or elsewhere in New Mexico against Canby's combined forces. Yet when General Sibley called for a council of war to deal with the "what-now" question, none of the senior officers wanted to be the one who advised a retreat. Finally, after much discussion and no proposals, William "Gotch" Hardeman, newly promoted lieutenant colonel of the Fourth Regiment, mustered the courage to state the obvious: the enemy could reinforce quicker than the Confederates, and the sooner the army got away the better. Old Gotch's advice was promptly accepted, and the ignominious withdrawal began the next day.[37]

The retreat from New Mexico started poorly and got worse. On April 12, the Confederates evacuated Albuquerque with Sibley leading half of the force down the west bank of the Rio Grande to Los Lunas and Green leading the remainder of the men down the east bank to Governor Connelly's now-abandoned hacienda at Los Pinos.

On April 14, Canby, having been joined by Paul's northern command and having received word that the Confederates had evacuated Albuquerque, led the Union force south on an overnight march to Los Pinos. The following morning he surprised Green, fought with the Texans for a few hours, and then watched as the dispirited and outnumbered foes retreated across the river under the cover of a vicious spring dust storm. This engagement, the so-called Battle of Peralta, was the last significant Union-Confederate engagement in New Mexico.[38]

Canby, not wanting a pitched battle and not wanting to be responsible for feeding and caring for a large number of prisoners, elected simply to "herd" Sibley's disheveled army out of the territory, so he trailed along the east bank as Sibley and the Texans slogged down the west bank.

Near the confluence of the Rio Puerco and Rio Grande, Sibley reached another decision point. His men were in no shape to take on Fort Craig, especially with Canby dogging his rear. The only option was a detour along the eastern slopes of the San Mateo Mountains. This proved yet another disaster for the unfortunate Texans. The 109-mile route was sandy and nearly waterless and the men struggled, suffered, and some died before rejoining the Rio Grande well south of Fort Craig, near the junction of Alamosa Creek and the main river, some fifteen days later.[39]

At one point during the retreat, Sergeant Peticolas described the plight of the Texans as follows:

> No order was observed, no company staid [sic] together. The wearied sank down upon the grass, regardless of the cold, to rest and sleep; the strong with words of execration upon their lips, pressed feverishly and frantically on for water. Dozens fell in together and in despair gave up all hope of getting to water and stopped, built fires, and fell asleep.[40]

By early May the remnants of the once-proud Sibley Brigade began to stagger into Mesilla. The men of Texas who had marched north with such bravado and confidence in February had returned empty-handed, leaving almost a thousand of their comrades in graves, hospitals, and stockades to the north. The New Mexico Campaign was over.

10

Reprise

There used to be a roadside marker at Glorieta Pass that gave a brief account of the fighting there in March 1862 and concluded with the bold statement, "The battle saved the West for the Union." Perhaps if one accepted Trevanion Teel's claim that it was Sibley's plan to occupy California, then it could be argued that whatever caused Sibley to change his mind could be said to have saved the West. However, since neither Teel's story nor the subsequent logic are particularly compelling, we are led to consider the somewhat less grandiose suggestion that the Battle of Glorieta Pass is somehow analogous to Gettysburg.

In a sense, the engagement on March 28, 1862, at Pigeon's Ranch was the high-water mark of the Confederate campaign in New Mexico. Although it was not the northernmost point of advance (for that matter, neither was Gettysburg), it was the closest the Texans got to Fort Union, their ultimate objective. Consequently, despite the fact that the scale of Glorieta Pass was only about 1 percent of that of the epic battle in Pennsylvania, the analogy to Gettysburg has, for several writers, been irresistible. The problem is that the phrase "Gettysburg of the West" implies more than a high-water mark; it suggests not just a turning point, but a tactical failure (i.e., Pickett's charge) that resulted in an abrupt strategic reversal. Such was not the case at Glorieta Pass.

First of all, Glorieta Pass was by definition a tactical victory for the Confederates: they drove the enemy from the field of battle. Secondly the strategic shift due to Glorieta Pass cannot be called abrupt. It was not until two weeks after the battle that General Sibley decided to return to Texas, and his decision had much more to do with Canby's movement from the south than with the result of the fighting at Glorieta Pass. Furthermore, it is clear in retrospect that the campaign was all but lost well before Glorieta.

Indeed it is tempting to say that the New Mexico campaign was lost when the decision was made to bypass Fort Craig after the victory at Valverde; and this of course is tantamount to saying that General Sibley's enterprise in northern New Mexico had no chance from the beginning. Whereas the Army of Northern Virginia was riding high prior to Gettysburg, Sibley had enjoyed no such success as Lee's at Chancellorsville. Valverde earned the Confederates some glory, but the failure to capture Fort Craig spelled doom for the New Mexico campaign.

On the other hand, the Gettysburg moniker may have at least some superficial applicability. The Battle of Glorieta Pass lasted three days; Pigeon's Ranch was a high-water mark of sorts; the Federal lines there resembled a fishhook; and there is the analogous issue of allowing a crippled enemy to escape. Just as Meade was criticized for not challenging Lee's withdrawal from Gettysburg, so was Slough for his own retreat, and so was Canby for not forcing a general battle on the Rio Grande. All three Federal commanders, of course, had good reasons for their alleged timidity.

When we reject the phrases "Battle that saved the West" and "Gettysburg of the West," we are left asking the question, "What difference *did* Glorieta Pass make, or what difference might have been made if certain things had gone a little differently?"

For instance, suppose Scurry had not lost his supply train at Johnson's Ranch. Could the Texans have taken Fort Union? The answer is almost surely not. It would have been next to impossible for Scurry to overtake Slough and force another engagement before the Federals reached Fort Union. And taking the new "star" fort once it was regarrisoned was out of the question. The Confederates had no heavy artillery, but more importantly they had neither the time nor the provisions for anything like a siege. With Canby marching northward, the Texans would soon have had two Federal forces to deal with, and it is hard to imagine an outcome very different from the one that actually transpired.

Or what if someone other than Sibley had been in charge? The Texan soldiers were inclined to put the blame for the failure of the campaign squarely on their general's shoulders. They saw everything except the weather and the poor winter grass as Sibley's fault. The authors of the 1887–88 series carried by the *Overton Sharp-Shooter* wrote that Sibley was the "very last man on earth who ought to have been placed in command of that expedition."[1] He was old (forty-five), lazy, loose-tongued, and "had formed too intimate an acquaintance with 'John Barley Corn.'" John Baylor was even more direct: "General Sibley needs no information: it is enough for him to know that there is to be a quantity of whiskey used in the enterprise."[2]

As for Ochiltree's glowing description of the supposed success at Glorieta Pass, Baylor, a long-time enemy of Sibley's aide, also debunked his rhetoric and pomposity:

> [This] young friend of his . . . stuck a bunch of feathers in his coat-tail pocket and . . . the captain [Ochiltree] strutted himself to death. Peace to his ashes!

Trevanion Teel was kinder to his commanding officer but agreed that Sibley "was not a good administrative officer. He . . . was too prone to let the morrow take care of itself."[3] The point of both writers was that the men suffered greatly for want of supplies, and if Sibley had only moved faster, the Yankees might not have had time to move or destroy the quartermaster stores the Confederates were depending on. Teel went on to suggest that "had Colonel John R. Baylor continued to command, the result might have been different."

It is true that Baylor was anything but slow and indecisive. In fact the *Santa Fe Gazette* had called him the "fast man of Arizona."[4] No doubt Baylor would have given the Federals more of a run for their money (and supplies) both before and after Valverde, but it is unlikely that he could have reached Fort Union with a large enough force to take the post from Colonel Paul's command before the arrival of the Colorado Volunteers. Such an attempt would again have put the Confederates between two hostile forces, and this time they would be strung out and potentially more vulnerable to offensive action by Canby or Slough.

Supplies aside, both the *Overton Sharp-Shooter* and Major Teel acknowledged that bypassing Fort Craig was a crucial mistake, and they could not have put the blame for that decision entirely on their general. In council of war after the "victory" at Valverde the assembled Confederate officers agreed that the move northward was preferable to returning to either Mesilla or San Antonio. So the campaign continued and, as Davidson told it, the Texans "won every fight . . . but never reaped the fruits of a single victory."[5]

General Sibley offered no excuses and accepted no blame. In his summary report, he wrote to the adjutant general in Richmond, "As for the results of the campaign, I have only to say that we have beaten the enemy at every encounter." He asserted that his men were better armed, clad, and supplied than when they entered New Mexico, and he concluded the report "trusting that the management of this more than difficult campaign . . . may prove satisfactory to the President."[6]

In a personal letter to John McRae, father of the Federal captain who died defending his guns at Valverde, Sibley gave a simple reason for his "precipitate evacuation" of New Mexico: "My dear sir, we beat the enemy wherever we encountered them. The famished country beat us."[7]

The claim to have beaten the enemy at every encounter may sound inconsistent with so disastrous a campaign, but it comes close to the truth. In the two major battles, Valverde and Pigeon's Ranch, the Confederates were clearly the victors, having driven the foe from the field. At Albuquerque and Peralta, the Rebels could claim to have won by virtue of repelling attacks against their defensive positions. If Glorieta Pass is viewed as a single battle whose outcome was determined at Pigeon's Ranch, then perhaps the Confederates did win every time.

The Participants

Many of the officers and men who survived the Battle of Glorieta Pass would be heard from again—both during and after the War.

John Slough was recommissioned as a brigadier general and served at various posts in the east, including as commander of the Military District of Alexandria, Virginia. After the war he was appointed as chief justice of the Territory of New Mexico by President Andrew Johnson as part of his program to "reward heroes of the Union Army." In 1867 he was shot and killed by Colonel William Rynerson (a veteran of Carleton's California Column and a prominent Las Cruces Republican) in the La Fonda Hotel in Santa Fe following "bitter, slurring criticism of Rynerson's army career by Slough." Rynerson was acquitted by a San Miguel County jury after pleading self-defense.[8]

John Chivington remained in the Colorado Volunteers for the rest of the war and led the infamous and controversial attack on Black Kettle at Sand Creek on November 29, 1864. He was pilloried in the press and by former colleagues including Edward Wynkoop and Samuel Tappan for this alleged "massacre," although no formal charges were ever filed against him. He returned to the active ministry for a short while, but embittered at what he viewed as unjustified and vicious attacks on him and his men, he left Colorado for a time, but returned to the state in the late 1860s and lived there until his death in 1894.[9]

Edward Wynkoop was promoted to major following John Chivington's promotion to colonel. He served in the Colorado Volunteers for the remainder of the war and was Chivington's principal accuser during the Sand Creek hearings. He later served as Indian agent at Fort Larned, Kansas, and as warden of the New Mexico Territorial prison. He died in Santa Fe in 1891 at the age of fifty-five.[10]

After the war Samuel Tappan was appointed by General William Tecumseh Sherman to the Indian Pacification Commission, on which he served with distinction. During that time, he met Henry M. Stanley, and it was through Tappan's good offices that that explorer was introduced to the benefactor who sent him to Africa to find Dr. Livingstone. Tappan spent his last years in Washington, D.C., where he died in 1913 at the age of eighty-three. He is buried in Arlington National Cemetery.[11]

Jacob Downing served in the Colorado Volunteers until the end of the war, then returned to the Denver area where he sold real estate until his death. Perhaps his most enduring legacy was the introduction of alfalfa to Colorado farmers from seeds he obtained during his stay in New Mexico.[12]

On the Confederate side, Henry Sibley left the country after the war and, together with a number of other high-ranking Confederate officers, tried to help the Khedive of Egypt organize his army. Unsuccessful in his attempt, due to fiscal mismanagement and his continuing penchant for the bottle, he returned to Fredericksburg, Virginia, where he died penniless in 1886.[13]

William Read Scurry was promoted to brigadier general in September 1862 and continued to fight for the Confederacy. He bled to death at the Battle of Jenkins Ferry in April 1864 after refusing to allow attendants to take him to the rear for treatment of his wounds.[14]

Charles Pyron continued to serve with the Sibley Brigade throughout the remainder of the war. He was wounded at the Battle of La Fourche and eventually attained the rank of colonel. After the war he returned to ranching near San Antonio and amassed a large fortune in the short time before his death in 1868 at the age of fifty-two.[15]

John Phillips survived his service in Sibley's Brigands only to be killed in San Antonio, Texas, in September 1862. Appropriately enough, the leader of the "Santa Fe Gamblers" was shot by Major Sherod Hunter, another Confederate officer, in a fight that resulted from a "paltry quarrel" over a game of cards.[16]

Alfred Peticolas, the tireless diarist, served out the war with the Sibley Brigade in Louisiana and returned to South Texas where he served as a prominent attorney and judge until his death in 1915 at the age of seventy-six.[17]

William "Old Bill" Davidson, of *Overton Sharp-Shooter* fame, was wounded for the third time at Peralta but stayed with the Brigade to participate in the recapture of Galveston and the campaign in Louisiana. Wounded yet twice again, he came out of the war with the rank of lieutenant colonel and returned to Richmond, Texas, to take up a highly successful law practice, one that was interrupted by several terms in public office.[18]

The Field of Battle

And what of Glorieta Pass itself—how has the battlefield weathered the 136 years since the bloody events of 1862? The railroad came in 1880, crossing the southern edges of both the Apache Canyon and Pigeon's Ranch battlefields. The Santa Fe Trail was eventually paved as US 85 and then Interstate 25, passing north of the Apache Canyon site and across the southern edge of the field where so many fell on March 28.

The three ranches—Kozlowski's, Pigeon's, and Johnson's—have endured with varying degrees of success. Johnson's Ranch is completely gone; a single building and the famous old well are all that remain of Alexander Valle's establishment; and Kozlowski's estate has survived several owners, most recently the much-acclaimed actress, Greer Garson.

A Lingering Question

The Battle of Glorieta Pass was back in the news in the summer of 1987 when thirty-one skeletons were found in shallow graves during excavation for the foundation of a new house. The discovery of the supposed Confederate burial site created a stir in the archeological and historical communities, and after several years of forensic analysis and a long

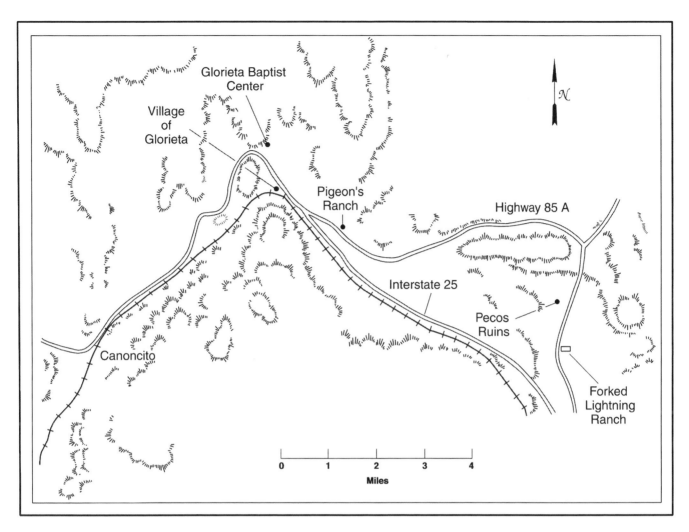

Glorieta Today
(Graphics by David Cunnington)

squabble over the proper reburial site, the soldiers' remains were finally reinterred in the Santa Fe National Cemetery in June 1993.[19]

There were questions, however. William Whitford, who visited the battleground several times around the turn of the century with veterans of the fight and whose book is illustrated with his own photographs, was very specific about the location of the graves of both the Union and Confederate dead. The Confederates, he said, were buried "just west of the ranch, and close to the high ledge of rocks [Sharpshooter's Ridge].

... The Union dead ... were interred in the open field to the east of Pigeon's Ranch."[20] The burial site discovered in 1987 was in an *open field east* of Pigeon's Ranch!

Whitford was simply mistaken, said the experts; it happens all the time. Then came the next question: What about the buckshot found among skeletal remains? Weren't the Texans the ones who were armed with shotguns? Well yes, that was a surprise, but there are several possible explanations. The shotguns may have been grabbed by the Union soldiers.[21]

"Someone has a strange concept of the hazards of removing a loaded, double-barreled shotgun from the hands of a moderately competent soldier," responded one of the skeptics.

What about uniforms? There were some uniform parts, including four belt buckles stamped "US," but some of the uniforms worn by Sibley's men were probably confiscated from the enemy as was vividly demonstrated by Peticolas's encounter with Tappan on the twenty-eighth. Besides, the fact that relatively few of the remains had associated uniform artifacts would indicate they were *not* those of Federal soldiers.

Then there was the separate grave containing the skeleton of a tall, well-built man of age twenty-eight to thirty-four, with trauma to the skull. Surely that was Major Shropshire. This would seem to be a good bet, except that according to another report on that particular skeleton, there was "no detectable trauma; however skull missing (hit by backhoe)"[22] and another report shows only a few fragments of skull, although it notes "radiating fractures and exit wound ... resulting from gunshot wound to the face."[23]

And around it goes. Resolution of the question is beyond the scope of this book, and may be unnecessary inasmuch as the large majority of people who are interested have accepted the Confederate identification. The soldiers' remains were reinterred in a nineteenth century military ceremony, with Texas and Confederate flags flying in the Santa Fe breeze.

Summary and Conclusion

On March 26, 1862, about seven hundred men, mostly from Colorado and Texas, had a brief skirmish near the western end of Glorieta Pass in north central New Mexico. Only a few soldiers were killed or injured but

Reburial of the Confederate dead at the Santa Fe National Cemetery (photograph by Thomas Edrington)

the Union forces drove the Confederates from the field and captured about one quarter of their force.

Two days later, on March 28, road-weary troops, now reinforced to total about fifteen hundred Federals and Confederates, again collided four miles further east along the Santa Fe Trail. This time the Texans won, but the fight left 250 young men killed or wounded on the battlefield. What's more, the Texans' seventy-wagon supply train was overrun and burned, leaving them without food or blankets in an early spring snowstorm. So just as at Valverde, only one month earlier, the Texans were victorious on the battlefield but were in serious trouble for want of food and supplies. This time, however, their quest for supplies turned them away from, not toward, their enemy and became the first step in what would eventually become a costly and inglorious retreat to their Texas homeland.

All battles, indeed all wars, have some element of futility and needless suffering, but Glorieta seems to have had more than its share. Consider that even if Chivington had not destroyed the wagon train, the outcome would have been the same—Sibley's New Mexico adventure was doomed to failure. Thus in the final analysis, the Battle of Glorieta Pass might best be viewed as little more than a bloody postscript to a star-crossed campaign.

This, then, is the legacy of Glorieta Pass—not a Gettysburg in the West, but a hollow and bloody addendum to a campaign whose outcome had already been decided.

Appendix

Union and Confederate Order of Battle, Unit Strengths, and Casualties at the Battle of Glorieta Pass

The Battle of Glorieta Pass comprised three engagements. The first occurred on the afternoon of March 26 in Apache Canyon; the second on March 28 in and around Pigeon's Ranch; and the third on the afternoon of March 28 in and around Johnson's Ranch. Since these engagements were geographically disconnected, this appendix describes their orders of battle and casualties separately.

Apache Canyon, March 26, 1862
Federal Order of Battle[1]

Regiment	Co.	Commander	Strength
Overall Command		Chivington	418
First Colorado			268
	A	Wynkoop	60
	D	Downing	60
	E	Anthony	60
	F	Cook	88
Third US Cavalry			100
	Var.	Howland	50
	E	Walker	50
First US Cavalry			
	D,G	Lord	50
(NM Vols		Chaves	30?[2])

Federal Casualties[3]

First Colorado	
Company A	
Wounded	CPL John Clinton
	PVT David Dunpiere
Company D	
Killed	PVT William G. Edwards
Wounded	SGT M. E. Boyle
	PVT John Keller
Company F	
Killed	PVT Martin Dutro
	PVT Jude W. Johnson
	PVT George Thompson
	LT William F. Marshall (mortally wounded)
Wounded	PVT Charles H. Bristol
	CPT Samuel H. Cook
	PVT William F. Hall
	PVT Jesse F. Kiehl
	PVT C. W. Logan
	PVT M. A. Patterson
	PVT A. B. Pratt
First US Cavalry	No casualties reported
Third US Cavalry	No casualties reported
New Mexico Volunteers	No casualties reported

Note that Hollister states that three Federal prisoners were also taken.[4]

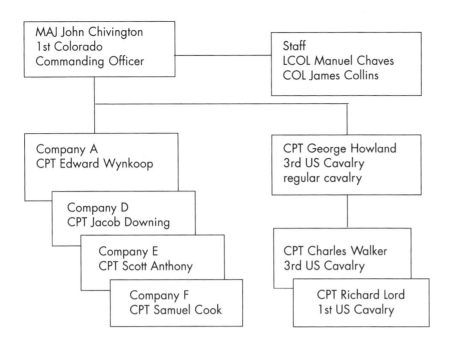

MAJ John Chivington
1st Colorado
Commanding Officer

Staff
LCOL Manuel Chaves
COL James Collins

Company A
CPT Edward Wynkoop

CPT George Howland
3rd US Cavalry
regular cavalry

Company D
CPT Jacob Downing

Company E
CPT Scott Anthony

Company F
CPT Samuel Cook

CPT Charles Walker
3rd US Cavalry

CPT Richard Lord
1st US Cavalry

**Union Order of Battle
March 26, 1862
Apache Canyon**

Summary of Federal Casualties at Apache Canyon,
March 26, 1862

Regiment	Company	K/MW	W[5]	P	Total
First Colorado		5	11(14)	3	19(22)
	A		2		
	D	1	2		
	F	4	7		
US Cavalry	no casualties reported				
NM Volunteers	no casualties reported				
	Grand Total	5	11(14)	3	19(22)

Confederate Order of Battle

Although the authors have not been able to account for all members of the eight companies that made up Pyron's command on March 26, a number of about 280 is thought to be reasonably accurate. Official Confederate reports do not give a number, but as shown below, there is considerable evidence to support a figure between 250 and 300.[6]

Writer	Rgt/Co	Date	2nd Rgt	5th Rgt	Total
Davidson	5/A	c.1888			300
Giesecke	4/G	March 1862			250
Hanna	4/C	March 1862			300
Hoffman	7/B	May 1862			150
Howell	5/C	May 1862		150	
McCown	5/G	May 1862	200		
McLeary	5/A	c.1895			250
Peticolas	4/C	March 1862			350
Williams	4/E	March 1862			170
Walker	Fed.	March 1862			250–300
Santa Fe Gazette		April 1862	80	200	280

Of the nine Confederates who reported numbers, Davidson and McLeary were participants. Giesecke, Hanna, Hoffman, Peticolas, and Williams were part of the command under Scurry that came to Pyron's relief on the night of the battle; hence they probably had good secondhand information. Davidson wrote that Pyron's men and Scurry's reinforcements sat up all night talking "like a bunch of girls." The following summary is the basis for the text:

Regiment	Co.	Commander	Strength
Overall Command		Pyron	281
Pyron's Battalion (Second Texas)			81[7]
	B	Jett	
	E	Stafford	
	Arty	Nettles	
	Brigands	Phillips	11[8]
Fifth Texas		Shropshire	200
	A	Wells	
	B	Scott	
	C	Shannon	
	D	Ragsdale	

Second Texas
    Company B   no casualties reported[10]
    Company E
        Prisoners   PVT Joseph Tate[11]
    Artillery   no casualties reported
    Brigands
        Killed   PVT Thomas Cator (mortally wounded)
        Prisoners   2LT John McIntyre
                  PVT J. P. Hanson (San Elizario Spy Company)

Fifth Texas
    Company A[12]
        Killed   PVT Samuel Terrell (mortally wounded)
        Prisoners[13]   2nd CPL Iredell Taylor
                  SGT Lovard Tooke
                  Blacksmith Andrew Galilee
                  PVT John Allen
                  PVT F. E. Caldwell
                  PVT Jacob Dick
                  PVT James Gilber
                  PVT Thomas Goode
                  PVT Abraham Griffits
                  PVT George Guinn
                  PVT Thomas Henderson
                  PVT William Henderson
                  PVT S. T. Kindred
                  PVT John Landrun *
                  PVT William Landrun *
                  PVT Ell Matthews
                  PVT James McLeary
                  PVT C. A. Micke
                  PVT William Newsome
                  PVT August Schubert
                  PVT Peter Silvey *
                  PVT John Starrett

PVT Charles Steadman *
PVT J. W. "Wat" Tinkler
PVT J. K. Vanarsdell *
PVT George Waddill *
PVT D. L. "Doc" Walker *
CPT Stephen Wells
PVT John Wenfree *

Company B
    Prisoners   PVT Thomas Logan
                  PVT Francis Oakes
                  PVT James Wright

Company C
    Wounded   PVT Perry Sapp (also captured)
    Prisoners   PVT Frank Camp
                  PVT Moses Camp
                  PVT Frank Coffield
                  PVT Paul DeCarpio
                  PVT Samuel Fulson
                  PVT Herman Giessel
                  PVT Henry Kernole *
                  PVT Henry Maywald
                  PVT James Nash
                  PVT Jonathan Nichols
                  PVT Joseph Pearson *
                  PVT Adolph Reicherzer
                  PVT William Stewart
                  PVT John Sullock[14]
                  PVT Moses Whitly

Company D
    Killed   PVT James McKinney
    Prisoners   2LT Felix Roan
                  1CPL Napoleon Odom
                  PVT Louis Krempkan *
                  PVT George Loe
                  PVT John A Lorentz *
                  PVT A.W. Prithen
                  PVT Samuel Wright

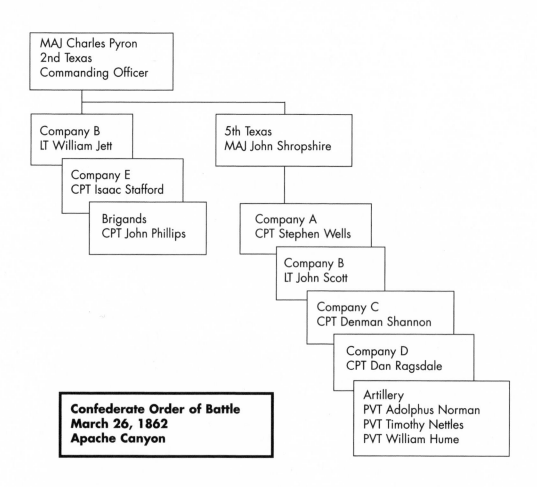

MAJ Charles Pyron
2nd Texas
Commanding Officer

Company B
LT William Jett

Company E
CPT Isaac Stafford

Brigands
CPT John Phillips

5th Texas
MAJ John Shropshire

Company A
CPT Stephen Wells

Company B
LT John Scott

Company C
CPT Denman Shannon

Company D
CPT Dan Ragsdale

Artillery
PVT Adolphus Norman
PVT Timothy Nettles
PVT William Hume

**Confederate Order of Battle
March 26, 1862
Apache Canyon**

Summary of Confederate Casualties at Apache Canyon, March 26, 1862

Regiment	Company	K/MW	W	P	Total
Second Texas		1		3	4
	B	no casualties reported			
	E			1	
	Arty	no casualties reported			
	Brigands	1		2	
Fifth Texas		2	1	55	58
	A	1		29	
	B			3	
	C		1	15+1	
	D	1		7	
unidentified units				13	13
	Grand Total	3	1[15]	71[16]	75

Pigeon's Ranch, March 28, 1862 Federal Order of Battle

Regiment	Co.	Commander	Strength	
Overall Command		Slough	884	
First Colorado		Tappan[17]	619[18]	
	C	Sopris		
	D	Downing		
	F	Nelson		
	G	Wilder		
	I	Kerber		
	K	Robbins		
Third US Cavalry	Var	Howland	100[19]	
First US Cavalry	D,G	Lord	50[20]	
Regular Artillery			85	
		Ritter	53[21]	two 12-pounders, two 6-pounders
		Claflin	32[22]	four 12-pounder mountain howitzers
US Quartermaster Corp.		Enos		100-wagon train
		"Police guard"	70[23]	

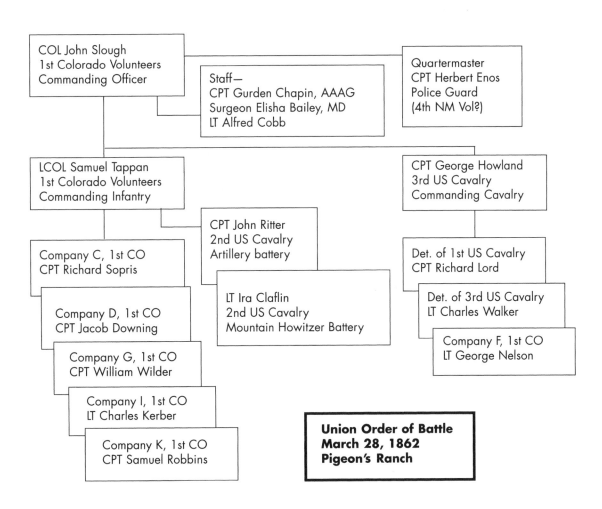

COL John Slough
1st Colorado Volunteers
Commanding Officer

Staff—
CPT Gurden Chapin, AAAG
Surgeon Elisha Bailey, MD
LT Alfred Cobb

Quartermaster
CPT Herbert Enos
Police Guard
(4th NM Vol?)

LCOL Samuel Tappan
1st Colorado Volunteers
Commanding Infantry

CPT George Howland
3rd US Cavalry
Commanding Cavalry

CPT John Ritter
2nd US Cavalry
Artillery battery

Company C, 1st CO
CPT Richard Sopris

Det. of 1st US Cavalry
CPT Richard Lord

LT Ira Claflin
2nd US Cavalry
Mountain Howitzer Battery

Company D, 1st CO
CPT Jacob Downing

Det. of 3rd US Cavalry
LT Charles Walker

Company G, 1st CO
CPT William Wilder

Company F, 1st CO
LT George Nelson

Company I, 1st CO
LT Charles Kerber

**Union Order of Battle
March 28, 1862
Pigeon's Ranch**

Company K, 1st CO
CPT Samuel Robbins

First Colorado					
Company C					Peter Johnson
Killed	Frank Billard				Patrick Keegan
	Hopkins M. Boon				Joseph King
	H. L. Moody				John Kohler
	J. Ochil				Matthew Laughlin
	Amos R. Peters				John Newcomer
	Andrew Points				George Owens
	Jacob Smith				Edward Prickett
Wounded	William Baldwin				John Snyder
	John Callery				Charles E. Wilbur
	LT Clark Chambers			Prisoners[25]	Jesse Hair
	John C. Fihlhauser				Charles Thomas
	Barton S. Mulkey				Benedict Olson
	Isaac N. Pierce			Company E[26]	
	Philip Rail			Wounded	W. Burk
	John T. Schneider				W. Ferguson
	Joseph V. Tosh				C. Mahan
	Willis Wilcox				J. Parker
	Richard Yates			Company F	
Company D				Wounded	Benjamin F. Ferris
Killed	Christopher Anderson				O. I. Freeman
	Charles Barton				Ed C. Gould
	Michael E. Boyle			Company G	
	Charles F. Creitz			Killed	Christian Butler
	Alfred J. Davis				Jarrett Hutson
	A. J. Denny				Harmon Lovelace
	John B. Elliott				O. C. Seymour
	Charles Fenner			Wounded[27]	William S. Clisbee
	William James				William G. Ford
	John J. McMillan				Edward F. Johnson
	J. G. Seeley				William Muxlow
	John E. Shepherd				David J. Osborn
	Adam Schuler				Edward W. Osborne
	Ilzatus Slawson			Prisoner	Michal Bacus[28]
	Matthew Stone			Company I	
Wounded	Benjamin Baker			Killed	LT John Baker
	John W. Davis				Samuel Bird
	Josiah D. Downing				John Freres
	William Elliott				John Garwick
	George W. Fall				Jasper Hotchkiss
	John F. Fleming				Henry Hirshhausen
	Joseph Flinn				Gotlieb Hittig
	Talmadge O. Foote				Lyman Honeywell
	Edwin B. Griffin				SGT William H. Hurst
	Thomas J. Hawes				Armand Johnson
	Charles D. Hicks				John Kreider
	William Iler				Ignatz Mattaush
					John Renderly

Federal Casualties (continued)

			Wounded	W. T. Cushman
Wounded	Frederick Rufer			James Donaldson
	John H. Stewart			William F. Eichbaum
	—— Austin			James Grealich
	Henry Backus			Oren H. Henry
	August Bartlett			Angus McDonald
	William Bowmand			H. H. Oren
	Frank Brass			Thomas H. Wales
	William Cudmore		Prisoners[31]	Lewis Percival
	James Doyle			Ward W. Dennison
	Austin Gerard	Company unknown		
	John Henry	Deserted[32]	—— Jones
	—— Houston		—— Miller
	Henry Johnson	Regular Artillery[33]		
	Henry Kemball	Ritter's Battery		
	O. McHenry	Killed	LT Peter McGrath
	Frederick Meggers[29]		George H. Smith (5/E)
	George Niedhardt	Wounded	—— Leddy (2nd Cav/I)
	Ole Oleson		—— Raleigh (5/E)
	Frederick Rafer		—— Woolsey (5/E)
	John Smith	Claflin's Battery	
	Peter Ward	Killed	Francis Richards (5/G)
Prisoners	5 unnamed[30]		John M. Smith (1st Cav/G)
		Wounded	John Noble
Company K			B. Doyle
Killed	H. C. Hanley	Third U.S. Cavalry	
	Moses Jones	Wounded	Arthur Selby (3/E)[34]

Summary of Federal Casualties at Pigeon's Ranch, March 28, 1862

Regiment	Company	K/MW	W	P	Desert.	Total
First Colorado		43	72	11	2	128
	C	7	11			
	D	15	21	3		
	E		4			
	F		3			
	G	4	6	1		
	I	15	19	5		
	K	2	8	2		
	Unk				2	
Artillery	Ritter	2	3			5
	Claflin	2	2		·	4
Third Cavalry			1			1
	GRAND TOTAL	47	78	11	2	138

Confederate Order of Battle

The number of men under the command of Colonel Scurry at Pigeon's Ranch has been the object of significant controversy over the years. General Sibley wrote on March 31 that Scurry had 1,000 men at Glorieta Pass,[35] while Scurry reported the same day with reference to his command at Pigeon's Ranch "from details and other causes they were reduced until (all combined) they did not number over 600 men fit for duty."[36] If both reports are assumed to be accurate, it remains to account for the difference of 400.

McLeary glossed over the discrepancy with the statement that Scurry had about 1,000 men; but, owing to the number on detail and sick and disabled, only about 600 were fit for duty and actively engaged.[37] This is enough like Scurry's original report that it is probably based on knowledge of that document. Accounts by Holcomb and Hoffman, which also support the number of 600, may also have been influenced by prior knowledge of Scurry's report, although Hoffmann, by virtue of commanding a battalion at Pigeon's Ranch, would have been in a position to know the correct number.[38]

A careful analysis of Hall's data suggests that there were between 1,000 and 1,100 men available to the northern wing of the Army.[39] This takes into account losses at Valverde and Apache Canyon, estimates of numbers of men in hospitals at Socorro, Albuquerque, and Santa Fe and the known deployments in Albuquerque and Cubero. There are several reports, as described later in this appendix, of approximately 200 men at Johnson's Ranch, and several of Scurry's officers (Jordan, Wright, Oakes, McGuiness, and Bennett) appear to have been elsewhere on the twenty-eighth. Some of these officers may have had detachments with them, but it is still difficult to account for the remaining 200 men. It might be tempting to accept Davidson's account which stated that "Glorieta will today be forced by 800 Texans,"[40] were it not for the question of whether or not "Old Bill" was including both Scurry's force and the men who remained behind at Johnson's Ranch.

Perhaps a third of the missing 200 can be accounted for by Sibley's not having the casualty figures from Apache Canyon when he reported that Scurry's command numbered 1,000. The fact that the report did not even mention Apache Canyon lends credence to this possibility.

Rafael Chacon reported that he escorted 500 prisoners, including about 200 wounded and "350 we had taken at Algodones," to Fort Union in mid-April.[41] One might wonder if these numbers could account for the missing 200 men, except that we have found no corroboration of Chacon's story nor any suggestion of the identity of the prisoners.

After much analysis, we find no compelling reason to contradict Scurry's cited numbers. He would seem to gain nothing from understating his forces when many others could have confirmed his error and there is no evidence that any of his colleagues did so. For that reason, we have chosen to use 600 men as the size of Scurry's force at Pigeon's Ranch.

Regiment	Company	Commander	Strength
Overall command		Scurry	600
2nd Texas		Pyron	77[42]
	Arty	Bradford	15(?)
	(three 12-pounder mountain howitzers)		
	Brigands	Phillips	8[43]
4th Texas		Raguet	260(?)
	B	Holland	
	C	Hampton	
	D	Lesueur	
	E	Buckholts	
	F	Crosson	
	G	Giesecke	
	H	Alexander	
	I	Odell	
	K	Foard	
5th Texas		Shropshire	129
	A	Carson	
	B	Scott	
	C	Shannon	
	D	Ragsdale	
7th Texas		Hoffman	120(?)
	B	Schwarzhoff (?)	
	F	Wiggins	
	H	Adair	
	I	Gardner	

Second Texas
Artillery
Wounded   2LT James Bradford
    PVT Frank Boone
    CPL William Carter
    PVT Adolph Hermann
    PVT Arthur White
Brigands
Killed   PVT Richard Tart
Wounded   PVT William Kirk
Prisoner   1LT George Madison
Fourth Texas
Staff
Killed   MAJ Henry Raguet
Wounded   Adjutant Ellsberry Lane
Company B
Killed   PVT Everett Foley
    PVT James McCord
Wounded   Blacksmith James Stroud
    PVT James Byars (also captured)
    PVT Pleasant A. Crawford
    PVT J. E. Standefer
Company C
Killed   PVT Ebeneezer Hanna (mortally wounded)
    PVT Jacob Hensen
    PVT Alexander Montgomery
Wounded   2CPL Lovell Bartlett
    PVT Samuel Brown
    PVT Benjamin White
Company D
Killed   PVT Joseph Clinchey
    PVT E. R. Slaughter
    PVT James Stevens
    PVT Burton Stone
    PVT William Straughn
Wounded   3SGT Daniel Huffmann
    4CPL Samuel Hill
    PVT Elbert Carter
    PVT William Farmer
    PVT Jesus Flores
    PVT John Stokes
Company E
Killed   CPT Charles Buckholts
    Farrier Joseph G.H. Able
    PVT Richard Alday

    PVT J. S. L. Cotton
Wounded   PVT J. J. Young
Prisoners[45]   PVT D. S. Moore
    PVT P. W. Chadoin
Company F
Killed   PVT Reuben P. Bentley
    PVT John Martin
    PVT William McCormick
    PVT William Parson
Wounded   1SGT Edwin B. Adams
    4CPL John Poe
    PVT John Harbison
    PVT Augustus Matthews
    PVT William Matthews (also wounded at Valverde)
Prisoner   PVT Fields Voss
Company G
Killed[46]   5SGT Otto Schroeder
    PVT Christopher Gollmer
    PVT August Juhl
    PVT Fritz Schaefer
Wounded   2CPL August Anthor
    PVT John Hassler
    PVT Henry Ilse
Company H
Killed   2SGT John McKnight
    PVT Jesse Jones (mortally wounded)
Wounded   1SGT Albert Nelson
    PVT Alfred Griffith
    PVT Joseph Rogers
Company I
Killed   Blacksmith James Manus
    PVT F. J. Hopkins
    5SGT Thomas Wilson
    PVT G. W. Walker (mortally wounded)
    PVT T. A. Wright (mortally wounded)
Wounded   CPT James Odell
    1LT W. J. Jones
    PVT N. B. Marsh
    PVT John Shivers
Company K
Wounded[47]   LT Ramsey
    1LT Edward Robb
    PVT William Teer

	PVT Thomas Williams		PVT Henry Brown
Fifth Texas			PVT H. T. Sherwood
Staff		Artillery (combined with other brigade artillery)	
Killed	MAJ John Shropshire	Killed	PVT Edward Burrowes
Company A		Wounded	PVT Pat Dowd (also captured)
Killed	PVT S. C. Jones (mortally wounded)		PVT Eugene Phillipe
Wounded	PVT William Davidson (also captured)		PVT N. B. Roff (also captured)
	PVT George Seymour	**Seventh Texas**	
	PVT David Taylor	Company B	
Prisoners	1st SGT William Land	Killed	2SGT Stephen Marbach
Company B			PVT August Haberman
Killed	1CPL Benjamin Greely		PVT Frank Riedel
Wounded	PVT Andrew Nations	Wounded	3SGT Charles Hasenbeck
Company C			PVT Kasper Moos
Killed	PVT R. P. Catlett (mortally wounded)		PVT Fr. Penshorn
Wounded[48]	PVT William Cabeen (also captured)	Company F	
	2LT J. P. Clough	Wounded	4SGT Nathanial Hillin
	PVT M. T. DuBose (also captured)		PVT R. A. Heflin
	CPL J. K. Grisett	Company H	
	PVT Nicholas Bringle	Killed	CPT Isaac Adair (mortally wounded)
	PVT Henry Lawless		Bugler G. N. Taylor
Prisoners	CPT Denman Shannon		PVT William Booker
Company D			PVT Peter Hail
Wounded	2SGT Gustavus Schmeltzer		PVT Robert Walker
		Wounded	PVT Henry Cobb
		Prisoner	PVT J. H. Gibson
		Company I	
		Killed	2LT Charles Mills
			CPL William Langston

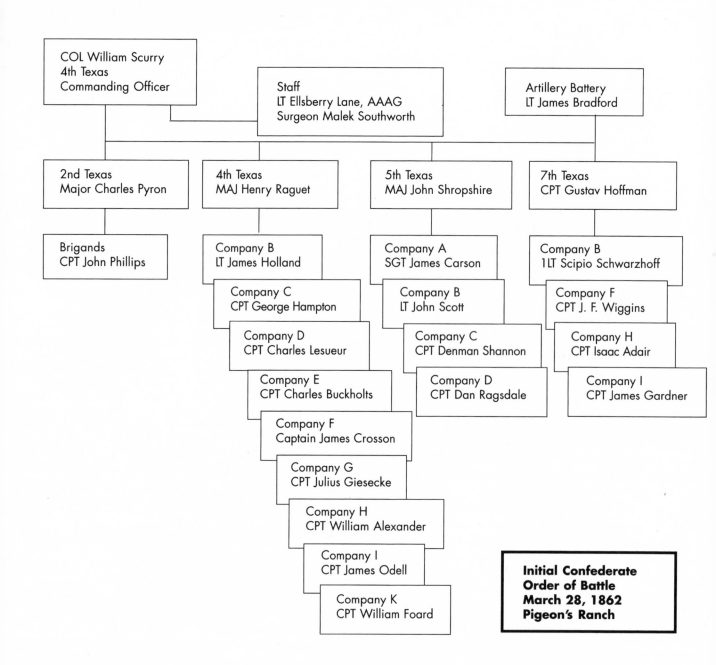

COL William Scurry
4th Texas
Commanding Officer

Staff
LT Ellsberry Lane, AAAG
Surgeon Malek Southworth

Artillery Battery
LT James Bradford

2nd Texas
Major Charles Pyron

4th Texas
MAJ Henry Raguet

5th Texas
MAJ John Shropshire

7th Texas
CPT Gustav Hoffman

Brigands
CPT John Phillips

Company B
LT James Holland

Company A
SGT James Carson

Company B
1LT Scipio Schwarzhoff

Company C
CPT George Hampton

Company B
LT John Scott

Company F
CPT J. F. Wiggins

Company D
CPT Charles Lesueur

Company C
CPT Denman Shannon

Company H
CPT Isaac Adair

Company E
CPT Charles Buckholts

Company D
CPT Dan Ragsdale

Company I
CPT James Gardner

Company F
Captain James Crosson

Company G
CPT Julius Giesecke

Company H
CPT William Alexander

Company I
CPT James Odell

Company K
CPT William Foard

**Initial Confederate
Order of Battle
March 28, 1862
Pigeon's Ranch**

Summary of Confederate Casualties at Pigeon's Ranch, March 28, 1862

Regiment	Company	K/MW	W	P	Total
Second Texas		1	2	2	5
	B			1	
	Brigands	1	2		
Fourth Texas		26	30+1	4	60
	Staff	1	1		
	B	2	4+1	1	
	C	3	3		
	D	5	6		
	E	4	1	2	
	F	4	5	1	
	G	2	3		
	I	5	4		
	K		3		
Fifth Texas		4	11+3	5	20
	Staff	1			
	A	1	3+1	2	
	B	1	1		
	C	1	4+2	3	
	D		3		
Seventh Texas		10	6	1	17
	B	3	3		
	F		2		
	H	5	1	1	
	I	2			
Artillery		1	6+2	2	9
Grand Total		42	55+6	14	111

Johnson's Ranch, March 28, 1862

Union Order of Battle[49]

Regiment	Company	Commander	Strength
Overall Command		Chivington	528
1st Battalion		Lewis	269
5th US Infantry			128
	A	Barr	
	G	Norvell	
1st Colorado			78
	B	Logan	
Ford's Independent Company			
(Company G, 4th New Mexico; may have included detachments from the 1st and 2nd Colorado)[50]			
		Ford	63
2nd Battalion		Wynkoop	219
1st Colorado			
	A	Shaffer	68
	E	Anthony	71
	H	Sanborn	80
Third US Cavalry			
	K	Falvey	40

Union Casualties

First Colorado			
	Company A	Wounded	PVT Simon Ritter
	Company B	No casualties reported	
	Company E	No casualties reported	
	Company H	No casualties reported	
Ford's Independent Company			
		Killed	CPL John Griffin (A/2nd CO) (mortally wounded)
5th US Infantry[51]			
	Company A	Wounded	PVT John Mayer
	Company G	Killed	PVT Francis Richards
		Wounded	PVT John Niblo
			PVT Richard McLeurty
			PVT Daniel Duggan

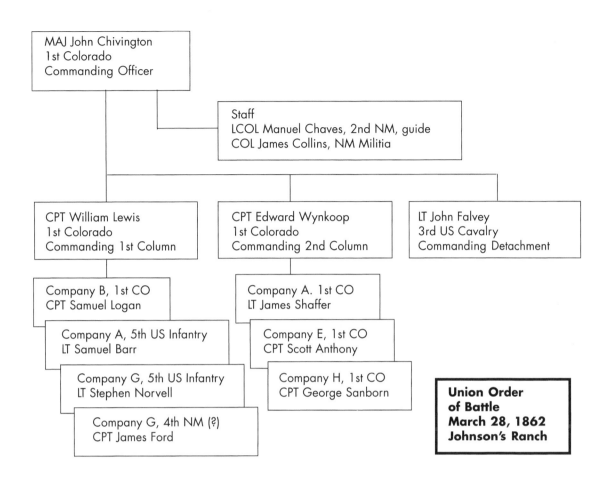

MAJ John Chivington
1st Colorado
Commanding Officer

Staff
LCOL Manuel Chaves, 2nd NM, guide
COL James Collins, NM Militia

CPT William Lewis
1st Colorado
Commanding 1st Column

CPT Edward Wynkoop
1st Colorado
Commanding 2nd Column

LT John Falvey
3rd US Cavalry
Commanding Detachment

Company B, 1st CO
CPT Samuel Logan

Company A. 1st CO
LT James Shaffer

Company A, 5th US Infantry
LT Samuel Barr

Company E, 1st CO
CPT Scott Anthony

Company G, 5th US Infantry
LT Stephen Norvell

Company H, 1st CO
CPT George Sanborn

Company G, 4th NM (?)
CPT James Ford

**Union Order
of Battle
March 28, 1862
Johnson's Ranch**

Summary of Federal Casualties at Johnson's Ranch,
March 28, 1862

Regiment	Company	K	W	P	Total
First Colorado					
	A		1		
	B	no casualties reported			
	E	no casualties reported			
	H	no casualties reported			
	Ford's Co.		1		
Fifth Infantry					
	A		1		
	G	1	3		
GRAND TOTAL		2	5		7

Confederate Order of Battle

Scurry did not say how many troops he left at Johnson's Ranch nor specifically if any particular units remained there. There were clearly wagonmasters and teamsters, wounded men, hospital attendants, cooks, and others including the chaplain. Given the fact that there were some prisoners, there were probably also some guards and there was a small artillery group with a single cannon.

By listing those companies that marched with him on the morning of March 28 and failing to mention Companies B and E of the Second Regiment, Scurry implied that those two companies were elsewhere, possibly at Johnson's.[52] The only reported casualty from these two units on the twenty-eighth was a private named Cavillo, who was captured, but it is not known where. On the other hand, the lack of organized resistance during Chivington's raid suggests that no substantial fighting units were present and Companies B and E may have been dispatched to Santa Fe on the twenty-seventh.

Whitford wrote that two companies of Germans, among others, were assigned to guard the wagons at Johnson's Ranch; but upon hearing the booming of cannon at Pigeon's Ranch, they left their post to join the fight.[53] There were in fact two German companies under Scurry's command (Company G of the 4th and Company B of the 7th); but there are several factors that cast serious doubt on Whitford's story. First, Scurry reported that these two units marched with him on the morning of the 28th. Second, the two units suffered casualties at Pigeon's Ranch to an extent somewhat above the average. Third, three members of these companies, including both captains, wrote about the fight on the twenty-eighth; and all three implied they were at Pigeon's Ranch from the outset. Indeed, no corroborating reports of Whitford's allegation have been found. In addition, it is questionable whether the twelve-pounders at Pigeon's Ranch could have been heard at Johnson's.

McLeary wrote after the war that the wagon guard consisted of about 200 sick and disabled men commanded by Chaplain Lucius H. Jones, although Scurry's report suggests that Lieutenant Taylor may have been the senior officer.[54] Two hundred may be high, but it is also the number given by Chivington, who although inclined to exaggerate, had the opportunity to get an accurate count while reconnoitering from the mesa.[55]

Other accounts are qualitative, suggesting "a lot" of sick, wounded, drivers, and cooks, and a "limited number" of effective combatants.

Based on this analysis, we assume that there were 200 Confederates at Johnson's Ranch on the twenty-eighth.

Regiment	Company	Commander	Strength
Overall Command		2LT John Taylor (?)	200
	Artillery (one 12-pounder howitzer)	PVT Timothy Nettles	6

Confederate Casualties

Second Texas			
	Company B[56]	Prisoner	PVT Pancho Cavillo
Fourth Texas			
	Staff	Wounded	Chaplain Lucius Jones (also captured)
	Company C	Prisoners	PVT C.B. Calender
			PVT Gideon Egg
			PVT John Warburton
	Company F	Prisoner	SGT Lucius Scott
	Company I	Killed	PVT J. K. Cruce
			PVT Rufus Ousley
Fifth Texas			
	Artillery	Wounded	PVT Timothy Nettles[57]
7th Texas		No casualties reported	
Seventeen unspecified prisoners are noted.			

Summary of Confederate Casualties at Johnson's Ranch, March 28, 1862

Regiment	Company	K/MW	W	P	Total
Various		2	2	17	21
	Grand Total	2	2	17	21

Notes

Chapter 1

1. Jerome C. Smiley used the phrase "Gettysburg of the Southwest" in his preface (written in June 1906) to William Clarke Whitford's *Colorado Volunteers in the Civil War* (Glorieta, New Mexico: The Rio Grande Press, 1971), 14.

2. Calvin Horn, *New Mexico's Troubled Years: The Story of the Early Territorial Governors* (Albuquerque: Horn and Wallace Publishers, 1963), 84–87. A detailed discussion of the politics in New Mexico before the war is in Loomis Ganaway's *New Mexico and the Sectional Controversy, 1846–1861* (Albuquerque: University of New Mexico Press, 1944). *Santa Fe Gazette*, May 11, 1861.

3. Darlis A. Miller, "Hispanos in the Civil War in New Mexico: A Reconsideration," *New Mexico Historical Review* 54, no. 2 (April 1979): 108.

4. B. Sacks, *Be It Enacted: The Creation of the Territory of Arizona* (Phoenix: Arizona Historical Foundation, 1964), 36; L. Boyd Finch, *Confederate Pathway to the Pacific: Major Sherod Hunter and Arizona Territory, C.S.A.* (Tucson: Arizona Historical Society, 1996).

5. Sacks, *Be It Enacted,* 58–60.

6. *The War of Rebellion: A Compilation of the Official Records of the Union and Confederate Armies,* 128 vols. (Washington, D.C., 1880–1901), series I, vol. 4, 35–78 (hereinafter noted simply as OR). Portions of the Official Records that pertain to the war in New Mexico were excerpted by Horn and Wallace and published in two vol-umes—*Confederate Victories in the Southwest* (Albuquerque: Horn and Wallace, 1963) and *Union Army Operations in the Southwest* (Albuquerque: Horn and Wallace, 1961).

7. *Journal of the Secession Convention of Texas, 1861* (Austin, 1912), 270; J. J. Bowden, *The Exodus of Federal Forces from Texas: 1861* (Austin: Eakin Press, 1986); Van Dorn to Ford, May 27, 1861, OR, I: 1, 577.

8. Martin Hardwick Hall, *The Confederate Army of New Mexico* (Austin: Presidial Press, 1978), 296–97.

9. Martin H. Hall, "Planter vs Frontiersman: Conflict in Confederate Indian Policy," in Frank Vandiver et al., eds., *Essays on the American Civil War* (Austin: University of Texas Press, 1968), 45–72, citing his own "Skirmish at Mesilla," in *Arizona and the West* 1 (Winter 1959): 344.

10. Jerry Don Thompson, *Colonel John Robert Baylor: Texas Indian Fighter and Confederate Soldier* (Hillsboro: Hill Junior College, 1971), 24.

11. Baylor to Washington, September 21, 1861, OR, I: 4, 17–19; Lynde to AAAG, July 26, 1861, OR, I: 4, 4–6.

12. Major James Cooper McKee, *Narrative of the Surrender of a Command of U.S. Forces at Fort Fillmore, New Mexico in July, A.D., 1861* (Houston: Stagecoach Press, 1960), 7.

13. Lynde to Canby, July 7, 1861, OR, I: 4, 59.

14. McKee, *Narrative of the Surrender.*

15. Finch, *Confederate Pathway,* 87, 89, 114.

16. Baylor to Van Dorn, August 25, 1861, OR, I: 4, 24.

17. Cooper to Sibley, July 8, 1861, OR, I: 4, 93.

18. Jerry Thompson, *Henry Hopkins Sibley: Confederate General of the West* (Natchitoches: Northwestern State University Press, 1987), 209.

19. Lewis F. Roe, "Recitals and Reminiscences: With Canby at Valverde," *National Tribune* (Washington, D.C.), Nov. 3, 1910 (courtesy Jerry Thompson).

20. Thompson, *Henry Hopkins Sibley*, 216–19.

21. Cooper to Sibley, July 8, 1861, OR, I: 4, 93.

22. Cooper to Van Dorn, July 9, 1861, as noted in Robert L. Kerby, *The Confederate Invasion of New Mexico and Arizona, 1861–1862* (Tucson: Westernlore Press, 1981), 146.

23. T. T. Teel, "Sibley's New Mexico Campaign—Its Objects and the Causes of Its Failure," in Robert U. Johnson and Clarence C. Buel, eds., *Battles and Leaders of the Civil War*, vol. 2 (1887; repr. Secaucus: Castle Press, n.d.), 700.

24. Teel, "Sibley's New Mexico Campaign"; Charles Walker, "Causes of the Confederate Invasion of New Mexico," *New Mexico Historical Review* 8, no. 2 (April 1933): 77–78; Martin H. Hall, "Colonel James Reily's Diplomatic Missions to Chihuahua and Sonora," *New Mexico Historical Review* 31, no. 3 (July 1956): 232–42. Finch, *Confederate Pathway*, 89; Stanley Zamonski, "Colorado Gold and the Confederacy," in Nauma L. James, ed., *The 1956 Brand Book of the Denver Posse of the Westerners* (Boulder: Johnson Publishing, 1957), 87–117; see also LeRoy Boyd, "Thunder on the Rio Grande, the Great Adventure of Sibley's Confederates for the Conquest of New Mexico and Colorado," *The Colorado Magazine* 24 (July 1947): 131–41.

25. Proclamation of Brigadier General H. H. Sibley, December 20, 1861, OR, I: 4, 90.

26. "Proclamation of General Kearny of 31 July" in Richard N. Ellis, ed., *New Mexico Historic Documents* (Albuquerque: University of New Mexico Press, 1975), 3.

27. William L. Davidson, "Green's Brigade, Reminiscences of the Old Brigade—On the March—in the Tent—in the Field as Witnessed by the Writers During the Rebellion, and Commanded by Generals Sibley, Green, and Hardeman, The Bravest of the Brave—A True History," The Overton, Texas, *Overton Sharp-Shooter* 2, no. 41, October 13, 1887.

Chapter 2

1. The best description of the Sibley Brigade is contained in Hall's *Confederate Army of New Mexico*. Much of the quantitative data in this work are taken from that source.

2. Hall, *Confederate Army*, 53–54; Ezra J. Warner, *Generals in Grey* (Baton Rouge: Louisiana State University Press, 1959), 270–71.

3. Odie Faulk, *Tom Green, Fightin' Texan* (Waco: Texian Press, 1963); Warner, *Generals in Grey*, 117–18; Hall, *Confederate Army*, 133–34.

4. The rest of the Seventh Texas remained in the El Paso–Mesilla area under the command of Colonel William Steele during the New Mexico incursion.

5. See Hall, "Planters vs. Frontiersmen," 51–62, esp. 54n. 37. For a detailed discussion of Baylor's relationship with Sibley and his exploits in Confederate Arizona see Finch, *Confederate Pathways*, 111, 171.

6. Hall, *Confederate Army*, 311–12.

7. Robert W. Frazer, *Forts of the West* (Norman: University of Oklahoma Press, 1965), 98; Marion Grinstead, *Life and Death of a Frontier Fort: Fort Craig, New Mexico* (Socorro: Socorro County Historical Society, 1973).

8. James W. Raab, *W. W. Loring: Florida's Forgotten General* (Manhattan, KS: Sunflower University Press, 1996); Warner, *Generals in Grey*, 193–94. Loring commanded a division at Vicksburg and fought against Sherman during the Atlanta Campaign. After the war he (along with Sibley and several other high-ranking Confederate officers) moved to Egypt where he rose to the rank of General of Division. He died in New York City in 1886.

9. Max Heyman, *The Prudent Soldier* (Glendale: Arthur H. Clark Publishers, 1959). Although the brother-in-law rumor was certainly untrue, suggestions that Canby was the best man at Sibley's wedding may have more credibility.

10. Horn, *New Mexico's Troubled Years*, 99, quoting "Territorial Papers of the U.S. Department of State, New Mexico, January 2, 1861–December 23, 1864," U. S. National Archives, Record Group 59 (hereinafter abbreviated NA RG).

11. Darlis Miller, "Hispanos and the Civil War," *New Mexico Historical Review* 54, no. 2 (April 1979): 105–23. For a discussion of the transfer of officers and men out of New Mexico see testimony of Colonel B. S. Roberts in "Report of the Joint Committee on the Conduct of the War," Senate Document 108, 37th Congress, 3d session, vol. 3 (1863), 364–72.

12. John Taylor, *Bloody Valverde: A Civil War Battle on the Rio Grande* (Albuquerque: University of New Mexico Press, 1995), 127.

13. Lee Meyers, "New Mexico Volunteers, 1862–1866," *The Smoke Signal* 37 (Spring 1979): 142–43.

14. Frazier, *Forts of the West*, 105–6. Although Fort Marcy in Santa Fe was technically the westernmost fort on the Santa Fe Trail, Fort Union was the last significant military post on that east-west trade route to the southwest.

15. Fort Union brochure; Frazer, *Forts of the West*, 105–6; Dale Giese, *Echoes of the Bugle, a Phelps-Dodge Corporation Bicentennial Booklet*, 1976, 10.

16. Post return for Fort Union, New Mexico, for March 1862 (NA RG 94). Numbers computed by evaluating numbers for "in garrison" and "detached," the latter mostly with Slough.

17. Taylor, *Bloody Valverde*, 146n1. Fort Conrad was built near the Valverde ford in 1851; but the swampy, malarial location was abandoned in 1854 in favor of Fort Craig, seven miles south. Frazier, *Forts of the West*, 97–98; Grinstead, *Life and Death of a Frontier Fort*.

18. The most thorough treatment of the Battle of Valverde is found in Taylor's *Bloody Valverde*, a companion to the present work.

19. Marion Grinstead, *Destiny at Valverde: The Life and Death of Alexander McRae* (Socorro: Socorro County Historical Society, 1992).

20. Thompson, *Henry Hopkins Sibley*, 259–61.

21. The Union forces lost 111 killed, 160 wounded, and 204 missing (most of whom were deserters): *Bloody Valverde*, 142.

22. The Confederates lost 72 killed and 157 wounded: *Bloody Valverde*, 136; Sibley to Cooper, May 4, 1862, OR, I: 9, 508.

Chapter 3

1. Theophilus Noel, *A Campaign from Santa Fe to the Mississippi, Being a History of the Old Sibley Brigade* (Houston: Stagecoach Press, 1961), 30; Sibley to Cooper, May 4, 1862, OR, I: 9, 508–9.

2. Sibley to Cooper, May 4, 1862, OR, I: 9, 509; *Overton Sharp-Shooter*, February 23, 1888.

3. Canby to AG, February 23, 1862, OR, I: 9, 633.

4. Donaldson was a member of the West Point class of 1836 and had been breveted to major for gallantry at the battle of Monterey. He eventually reached the brevet rank of major general of volunteers in 1865 for "faithful and meritorious service during the Rebellion" (George W. Cullum, *Biographical Register of the Officers and Graduates of the U.S. Military Academy at West Point* [Boston: Houghton, Mifflin, 1891], entry 856). Lord's and Howland's movements are discussed in testimony given at the Lord Court of Inquiry (Proceedings of a Court of Inquiry in the Case of Captain R. S. C. Lord, First U.S. Cavalry, by Headquarters, Department of New Mexico under Special Order no. 171, September 22, 1862, Ruhlen Collection, New Mexico State University); Canby to AG, February 23, 1862, OR, I: 9, 633; Paul to AG, March 11, 1862, OR, I: 9, 646.

5. Wesche to "General," May 5, 1862, OR, I: 9, 605–6; Don E. Alberts, ed., *Rebels on the Rio Grande: The Civil War Journal of A. B. Peticolas* (Albuquerque: University of New Mexico Press, 1984), 53; "Letter from Capt. McCown," *The*

Bellville Countryman, June 7, 1862; W. A. Faulkner, "With Sibley in New Mexico: The Journal of William Henry Smith," *West Texas Historical Association Year Book* 28 (October 1951): 135.

6. McCown to *Bellville Countryman*, June 7, 1862; Alberts, *Rebels,* 51; Connelly to Secretary of State, March 1, 1862, OR, I: 9, 638–39.

7. Martin Hall, "The Journal of Ebenezer Hanna," *Password* 3, no. 1 (January 1958): 24.

8. Noel, *A Campaign*, 33; Faulkner, "With Sibley in New Mexico," 137. Some of the buildings burned in Albuquerque belonged to Sophia Carleton, wife of Brevet Major (and later General and Departmental Commander of New Mexico) James Carleton (Giese, *Echoes,* 7). Enos to Donaldson, March 11, 1862, OR, I: 9, 527–28. Enos biographical information from Cullum, *Biographical Register,* entry 1758.

9. L. E. Daniell, *Texas: The Country and Its Men* (no publisher or date), 531; *Overton Sharp-Shooter,* May 17, 1888.

10. Thurmond to Officer Commanding C.S. Forces, March 19, 1862, OR, I: 9, 528–29; Enos to Donaldson, March 11, 1862, OR, I: 9, 527–28; Noel, *A Campaign,* 34; Giese, *Echoes,* 11.

11. Donaldson to Paul, March 10, 1862, OR, I: 9, 527; Connelly to Seward, March 11, 1862, OR, I: 9, 645; Sibley to Cooper, May 4, 1862, OR, I: 9, 509. F. S. Donnell, "When Las Vegas was the Capital of New Mexico," *New Mexico Historical Review* 18, no. 4 (October 1933): 266–72.

12. Donaldson to Paul, March 10, 1862, OR, I: 9, 527; Chaves affidavit in Compiled Service Record Of Manuel Chaves (NA, RG 94): Roster of men accompanying Manuel Chaves (compiled by Chuck Meketa).

13. Sibley to Cooper, May 4, 1862, OR, I: 9, 509; William Waldrip, "New Mexico During the Civil War," *New Mexico Historical Review* 28, no. 3 (July 1953): 252. Note that there is some dispute about whether or not Pelham was actually installed as territorial governor by Sibley—see Martin Hardwick Hall, *Sibley's New Mexico Campaign* (Austin: University of Texas Press, 1960), 168n. 12.

14. F. S. Donnell, "When Las Vegas was the Capital of New Mexico," 265–72.

15. Paul to AG, March 11, 1862, OR, I: 9, 645–46.

16. Robert M. Utley, *Fort Union* (Washington: National Park Service, 1962), 25.

17. Whitford, *Colorado Volunteers,* 38–39.

18. Ibid., 45, 50.

19. Ralph Emerson Twitchell, *The Leading Facts of New Mexican History,* vol. 2 (Albuquerque: Horn & Wallace, 1963), 382; Ovando J. Hollister, *Colorado Volunteers in New Mexico, 1862* (Chicago: R. R. Donnelley, 1962), 75–76; Gary Roberts, *Death Comes for the Chief Justice* (Niwot: University Press of Colorado, 1990).

20. Whitford, *Colorado Volunteers,* 43–44; Major John H. Nankivell, *History of the Military Organizations of the State of Colorado 1860–1934,* Part I (Denver: W. H. Kistler Stationary Co., 1935), 16.

21. Hunter to Acting Governor of Colorado, February 10, 1862, OR, I: 9, 630; Whitford, *Colorado Volunteers,* 75.

22. *Denver Post,* January 19, 1913. Both Tappan's father and brothers (Lewis and Arthur Tappan) were very active in the prewar abolitionist movement (James B. Stewart, *Holy Warriors-Abolitionists and American Slavery* [New York: Hill and Wang, 1976]).

23. Whitford, *Colorado Volunteers,* 77; Hollister, *Colorado Volunteers,* 73.

24. *The March of the First, Being a History of the Organization, Marches, Battles and Service of the First Regiment of Colorado Volunteers by a Private of the Regiment* (Denver: Thomas Gibson, 1863), 6.

25. Correspondence and editorials in the *Rocky Mountain News* on March 22, 1862, describe the "shame and disgrace" to the Territory caused by the foragers of the First Colorado.

26. *March of the First,* 7; Hollister, *Colorado Volunteers,* 79.

27. Hollister, *Colorado Volunteers,* 79, 83.

28. Ed. *Civil War Times Illustrated,* "The Pet Lambs at Glorieta Pass," *Civil War Times Illustrated* (November 1976), 32.

29. Ibid.

30. Sibley to Cooper, May 4, 1862, OR, I: 9, 509; *Overton Sharp-Shooter*, February 23, 1888, March 1, 1888, May 17, 1888.

31. Jerry D. Thompson, ed., *Westward the Texans: The Civil War Journal of Private William Randolph Howell* (El Paso: Texas Western Press, 1990), 95; Alberts, *Rebels,* 72; *Overton Sharp-Shooter*, Feb. 23, 1888, March 1, 1888, May 17, 1888.

32. *Overton Sharp-Shooter*, Feb. 23, 1888, March 1, 1888, May 17, 1888.

33. McCown to *Bellville Countryman*, June 7, 1862; *Overton Sharp-Shooter*, Feb. 23, 1888; Alberts, *Rebels,* 74.

34. Canby to AG, Feb. 23, 1862, OR, I: 9, 633; Paul to AG, March 11, 1862, OR, I: 9, 646.

35. Paul to AG, March 11, 1862, OR, I: 9, 646. Paul was ultimately breveted to brigadier general for gallantry at Gettysburg (Warner, *Generals in Blue,* 363–64).

36. Hollister, *Colorado Volunteers,* 86; Canby to Paul, March 16, 1862, OR, I: 9, 653.

37. Paul to Slough, March 22, 1862, OR, I: 9, 653; Paul to Slough, March 22, 1862, OR, I: 9, 654–55.

38. Paul to AG, March 24, 1862, OR, I: 9, 652.

39. Chapin to Paul, March 22, 1862, OR, I: 9, 654.

40. Chivington, "The Pet Lambs," *Denver Republican,* May 20, 1890.

41. *March of the First,* 8; Hollister, *Colorado Volunteers,* 93.

42. Canby to Slough, March 18, 1862, OR, I: 9, 649; Slough to AG, March 30, 1862, OR, I: 9, 534; Whitford, *Colorado Volunteers,* 82.

43. Reginald Craig, *Fighting Parson: A Biography of Colonel John M. Chivington* (Los Angeles: Westernlore Press, 1959), 40–41; Whitford (*Colorado Volunteers,* 52) also has some biographical information on Chivington.

44. Marc Simmons, *Following the Santa Fe Trail* (Santa Fe: Ancient City Press, 1984), 184. Alan J. Stewart, Lee D. Olson, eds., *Denver Westerners Golden Anniversary Brand Book 1991* 33 (Salt Lake City: Publishers Press, 1995), 196; Giese, *Echoes of the Bugle,* 12. Note that Stewart says that Kozlowski's first name was Martin. John D. Miller, letter to father, April 3, 1862, Arrott Collection, New Mexico Highlands University; Chivington to Canby, March 26, 1862, OR, I: 9, 530; Hollister, *Colorado Volunteers,* 93–94.

Chapter 4

1. *Santa Fe Weekly Gazette,* April 26, 1862; *Overton Sharp-Shooter*, May 17, 1888.

2. Alvin Josephy, *The Civil War in the American West* (New York: Alfred A. Knopf, 1991), 59.

3. Hall, *Confederate Army,* 373–74.

4. One of the unknowns of Glorieta has to do with Pyron and Shropshire's source of supplies. They had 280 men and had apparently left Santa Fe for good but there is no mention of a supply train.

5. Betsy Swanson, *The Glorieta Battlefield,* unpublished manuscript, September 1985, II–1 quoting Morris F. Taylor, *First Mail West, Stagecoach Lines on the Santa Fe Trail* (Albuquerque: University of New Mexico Press, 1971), 180.

6. Miller to father, April 3, 1862; *Overton Sharp-Shooter*, February 23, 1888; J. H. McLeary, "History of Green's Brigade," in Dudley G. Wooten, ed. *A Comprehensive History of Texas, 1685–1895,* vol. 2 (Dallas: William G. Scarff, 1898), 700; Hollister, *Colorado Volunteers,* 94.

7. Miller to father, April 3, 1862.

8. *Overton Sharp-Shooter*, February 23, 1888. This Union figure of 418 does not include Chaves's command of some thirty men of the Second New Mexico. Chaves stated that he joined Chivington at Pigeon's Ranch about March 22 and fought the Texans at Apache Canyon. Jacqueline Dorgan Meketa, ed., *Legacy of Honor: The Life of Rafael Chacon, A Nineteenth-Century New Mexican* (Albuquerque: University of New Mexico Press, 1986); Chivington to Canby, March 26, 1862, OR, I: 9, 53. Whereas the authors have not been able to account for all members of the

eight companies that made up Pyron's command on March 26, the total of 280 is thought to be reasonably accurate. See appendix.

9. Chivington wrote in his memoirs that his advance guard captured a lieutenant and thirty men on this occasion. Whitford repeated the story, but no other accounts nor Confederate casualty figures substantiate the claim. It is surmised that the lieutenant referred to was McIntyre, who was captured earlier that morning, and the number of prisoners grew from four to thirty with the passing of years. J. M. Chivington, "The First Colorado Regiment," *New Mexico Historical Review* 33, no. 2 (April 1958), 148; Hollister, *Colorado Volunteers,* 98; McLeary, *A Comprehensive History,* 700; Miller to father, April 3, 1862.

10. Hollister (*Colorado Volunteers,* 98) described the flag, but such a banner is not mentioned by Alan Sumrall in his "Battleflags of Texans in the Confederacy" (Austin: Eakin Press, 1995). In fact the only flag that can be firmly documented as being carried by the Sibley Brigade to New Mexico is the First National sketched by Peticolas in his diary (Alberts, *Rebels,* 100).

11. *Overton Sharp-Shooter,* February 23, 1888; Walker to Macrae, May 20, 1862, OR, I: 9, 531; Whitford, *Colorado Volunteers,* 88; *March of the First,* 8–9; Hollister, *Colorado Volunteers,* 99.

12. Walker to Macrae, May 20, 1862, OR, I: 9, 531; Chivington to Canby, March 26, 1862, OR, I: 9, 530; Miller to father, April 3, 1862; Whitford, *Colorado Volunteers,* 88–89; Kansas Historical Collection 13 (1913–14), 71–79 (Colorado Historical Society newsclipping file).

13. *Overton Sharp-Shooter,* February 23, 1888; McLeary, *A Comprehensive History,* 700; Walker to Macrae, May 20, 1862, OR, I: 9, 531.

14. Privates Nettles, Hume, and Norman were all from Company A of the Fifth Texas and were transferred to the Valverde Battery on June 1, 1862. Hume and Nettles also served in the Regimental Artillery, which must have been important, because they were promoted to first lieutenants of the Valverde Battery, while Norman, who seemed

to be in charge on March 26, remained a private. Davidson wrote that Lieutenant Jordan Bennett and Sergeant Joseph McGuiness of Teel's Artillery would have been in charge but were elsewhere that day (*Overton Sharp-Shooter,* March 8, 1888).

15. Miller to father, April 3, 1862.

16. Chivington to Canby, March 26, 1862, OR, I: 9, 531; Chivington, "The First Colorado," 149; Hollister, *Colorado Volunteers,* 100; Whitford, *Colorado Volunteers,* 90.

17. Whitford, *Colorado Volunteers,* 89; *Overton Sharp-Shooter,* Feb. 23, 1888; McLeary, *A Comprehensive History,* 700.

18. *Overton Sharp-Shooter,* February 23, 1888; Chivington to Canby, March 26, 1862, OR, I: 9, 531; Whitford, *Colorado Volunteers,* 92.

19. Hall, *Confederate Army,* 149; *March of the First,* 9.

20. Hall lists twenty-nine members of Company A who were captured; Davidson says the number was thirty-four. Hall, *Confederate Army; Overton Sharp-Shooter,* February 23, 1888.

21. *Overton Sharp-Shooter,* April 12, 1888; Slough to AG, March 30, 1862, OR, I: 9, 534.

22. Chivington, "The First Colorado," 149; Hollister, *Colorado Volunteers,* 101; Miller to father, April 3, 1862.

23. Hollister, *Colorado Volunteers,* 103–4; Miller to father, April 3, 1862.

24. *Overton Sharp-Shooter,* February 23, 1888.

25. *Overton Sharp-Shooter,* February 23, 1888, March 1, 1888; Chivington to Canby, March 26, 1862, OR, I: 9, 531; McLeary, *A Comprehensive History,* 700.

26. David Westphall, "The Battle of Glorieta Pass—Its Importance in the Civil War," *New Mexico Historical Review* 44, no. 2 (April 1969): 146.

27. Chivington, "The First Colorado," 149.

28. Whitford retold the story of Cook's men jumping the arroyo and included in his book a photograph of the "strategic bridge" (Whitford, *Colorado Volunteers,* 91). A bridge that still stands today served as a model for the painting shown in this work. The painting is by Willard Andrews

and was completed in the 1950s on a commission from James Toulouse (Ruth Armstrong, "Willard Andrews—For Love of New Mexico," *New Mexico Magazine* 60, no. 7 [July 1982]: 40–45). It is especially noteworthy that neither Hollister nor Miller, both of whom belonged to Company F and participated in the charge, mentioned the jump across the arroyo.

29. Miller to father, April 3, 1862.

30. Hanna reported four killed and six wounded; McLeary and Peticolas, two killed and three wounded; and Williams, two killed and five wounded. Hall indicates one killed, two mortally wounded, and one wounded. Some of the Confederate writings give fewer than the seventy-one prisoners claimed by Chivington. Hall lists fifty-eight. On the Federal side, Chivington gives five killed and fourteen wounded; Hollister, five killed, thirteen wounded, and three missing; and Slough five killed and eight wounded. By-name listings suggest five killed and eleven wounded. Hall, "Journal of Ebeneezer Hanna," 28; McLeary, *A Comprehensive History,* 700; Alberts, *Rebels,* 76; Connie O'Donnell, *The Diary of Robert Thomas Williams: Marches, Skirmishes, and Battles of the Fourth Regiment Texas Militia Volunteers, October 1861–November 1865,* typescript (Center for American History, University of Texas), 8; Hall, *Confederate Army;* Chivington to Canby, March 26, 1862, OR, I: 9, 531; Hollister, *Colorado Volunteers,* 107; Slough to AG, March 30, OR, I: 9, 534.

31. The term "devils from Pike's Peak" comes from a letter ostensibly written by a Confederate soldier named George Brown, who had allegedly been captured at Apache Canyon. Despite the generally peculiar character of the letter, several historians have quoted from it as if it were authentic. We would report here that (1) we have found no evidence of the existence of George Brown or any of the other three Texans mentioned in the letter, (2) the Coloradan mentioned did exist, (3) Brown's accounts of Confederate numbers, movements, and casualties are in error, and (4) what is said about Federal tactics at Apache Canyon is accurate. Therefore, the George Brown letter (which is reproduced in Hollister, *Colorado Volunteers,* 260–65) is almost surely a hoax, probably perpetrated by a member of the First Colorado Volunteers.

32. *Overton Sharp-Shooter,* February 23, 1888; McLeary, *A Comprehensive History,* 700.

Chapter 5

1. See appendix for list of casualties; Chivington, *The First Colorado Regiment,* 149.

2. Hall, *Sibley's New Mexico Campaign,* 142. There is some question about who was in command of the Seventh. According to Gustav Hoffmann (Oscar Haas, "Eggeling, Hoffmann Letters Describe New Mexico Battles," *New Braunfels Herald,* September 19, 1961), he led the four companies on the twenty-eighth, but Scurry's May 4 report suggests that Powhatan Jordan may have still been in charge on the twenty-sixth when they reached Galisteo. Scurry and the others did not clarify this situation in their official reports. The number of men who accompanied Scurry is discussed in the appendix.

3. *Overton Sharp-Shooter,* March 1, 1888.

4. Lansing Bloom, ed., "Confederate Reminiscences," *New Mexico Historical Review* 5, no. 3 (July 1930): 315–24 (Holcomb letter).

5. *Overton Sharp-Shooter,* May 17, 1888.

6. Ibid.

7. Whitford, *Colorado Volunteers,* 98.

8. *Overton Sharp-Shooter,* March 1, 1888.

9. Alberts, *Rebels,* 76. The steep traverse was necessary to bypass the short but virtually impassable gorge where Galisteo Creek runs from Apache Canyon to the plain to the south.

10. McLeary, *A Comprehensive History,* 701; Alberts, *Rebels,* 76; *Overton Sharp-Shooter,* March 1, 1888.

11. Whitford, *Colorado Volunteers,* 93.

12. Ibid. Whitford noted that "some of these skeletons had washed up 'recently'" (i.e., circa 1906).

13. Whitford, *Colorado Volunteers,* 96–97.

Alexander Valle's claim file in "Claims Considered under the Act of July 4, 1864 and Rejected—1875–1895, NA, RG92, files of the Quartermaster General, Box 148, package 49.

14. Bloom, *Confederate Reminiscences,* Holcomb letter; Scurry's report says that the wagon train took a route approximately six miles to the west (Scurry to Jackson, March 31, 1862, OR, I: 9, 541).

15. Whitford, *Colorado Volunteers,* 98.

16. Westphall (*Glorieta Pass,* 146) recalls the meager water supply.

Chapter 6

1. See Alexander Valle's affidavit dated July 25, 1870, and Chivington's letter in support of Valle's claim dated October 1870.

2. Scurry to Jackson, March 31, 1862, OR, I: 9, 542–44; Slough to AG, March 30, 1862, OR, I: 9, 534–36.

3. Slough lists the arrival time as 2:00 A.M. (Slough to AG, March 30, 1862, OR, I: 9, 534–36). Enos says that the command left Bernal Springs at 9:00 A.M. and arrived at Kozlowski's at 3:00 A.M. with only one halt (Enos to McFiman, April 5, 1862, NA, RG 42, Quartermaster General Consolidated File, Book 48, M430). In the same report he also notes that the distance from the Union camp at Bernal Springs to Pigeon's Ranch was thirty-four miles.

4. Slough to AG, March 30, 1862, OR, I: 9, 534–36; Slough's choice of the term "reconnaissance-in-force" in his after-action reports has been characterized by some as a self-serving attempt to put a positive spin on an embarrassing defeat.

5. Enos says that the entire command was preparing to move between 7:00 and 8:00 A.M. (Enos to McFiman, April 5, 1862) and Slough states that he "left the encampment" at 9:00 (Slough to AG, March 30, 1862, OR, I: 9, p 534).

6. The actual role of Slough's cavalry commander, Captain George Howland, in the engagement on the twenty-eighth is somewhat unclear. Tappan refers to the advance units as "Howland's

cavalry" (Tappan to Chapin, March 28, 1862, OR, I: 9, 536–38); and Howland himself says that he was "engaged . . . at and near the farm and premises of Alexander Valle at a place called La Glorieta." (Howland affidavit in Valle claim file, NA, RG92, op. cit.). However, Slough suggests that during the actual engagement the cavalry was commanded by Captain Gurden Chapin of the Seventh Infantry (Slough to AG, March 30, 1862, OR, I: 9, 534–36), and Captain Charles Walker does not refer directly to Howland's presence with the vanguard on the twenty-eighth, although he characterizes his overall operations on the twenty-sixth through twenty-eighth as "a part of the cavalry command under Capt. G. W. Howland" (Walker to Macrae, May 20, 1862, OR, I: 9, 531–32). Cullum, *Biographical Register,* entry 1774. See also note 24 below.

7. Enos to McFiman, April 5, 1862.

8. Cullum, *Biographical Register,* entries 1742 (Ritter) and 1786 (Claflin). Cannon that fired conventional solid cannonballs were traditionally referred to as "guns." They used a relatively flat trajectory for maximum effectiveness. Artillery pieces that were designed to fire shells were called howitzers. They were shorter-barreled than guns of equivalent shot weight, employed a lighter powder charge, and used a more elevated trajectory. Mountain howitzers were small twelve-pounders which were light enough to be completely disassembled and carried on three pack animals. In the field a mountain howitzer could be towed by a single animal. Ian Drury and Tony Gibbons, *The Civil War Military Machine* (New York: Smithmark Publishers, 1992), 66–81, and Dean S. Thomas, *Cannons—An Introduction to Civil War Artillery* (Gettysburg: Thomas Publications, 1985), 32.

9. Enos to McFiman, March 29, 1862, and April 5, 1862.

10. We have inferred that the train may have been escorted by the "seventy-man police guard" referred to by Tappan (Tappan to Chapin, May 21, 1862, OR, I: 9, 536). This group was probably composed of men from the First U.S. Cavalry and the Fourth New Mexico Volunteers because they

appear on the post return but are not mentioned as participating in the action (supplement to Fort Union post return, March 1862—see also Chapter 8, note 4). In addition, Whitford (*Colorado Volunteers,* 101) refers to a "broken company of New Mexican volunteers" at Pigeon's Ranch on the twenty-eighth. Although Enos says that there was "no escort" (Enos to McFiman, April 5, 1862), he may have been referring to a point later in the fight after the reserve had been moved up, away from the train. With the exception of the vanguard, the regular cavalry was not a factor in the fight, probably because the terrain was not suitable for fighting on horseback or even moving rapidly from place to place, except on foot, and so may have been left in the rear to escort the train. Walker notes that after he was withdrawn to a ridge behind Pigeon's Ranch early in the fight, he "accomplished nothing of special importance" (Walker to Macrae, May 20, 1862, OR, I: 9, 531–32). Farmer (J. E. Farmer Manuscript, 22) notes that when the Federals had fallen back to the third and final position near the train they were near a ravine where "we had two companies of dragoons under command of Captain Lord."

11. Enos to McFiman, April 5, 1862.

12. Scurry to Jackson, March 31, 1862, OR, I: 9, 542–44; Alberts, *Rebels,* 77; Harvey Holcomb makes the food comment and further notes that "we had a heavy guard all night" (Bloom, *Confederate Reminiscences,* 315–24).

13. In his March 31, 1862, report, Scurry notes that Lieutenant Taylor was in charge of the train (Scurry to Jackson, March 31, 1862, OR, I: 9, 542–44). The size of the Confederate train and its escort at Johnson's Ranch are also matters of some dispute. In his report (Chivington to AG, March 28, 1862, OR, I: 9, 538–39) Chivington says that eighty wagons were burned. Downing (*Rocky Mountain News,* June 7, 1862) says sixty, and Enos (Enos to McFiman, March 29, 1862) says "about fifty." In an affidavit in his compiled service record, Manuel Chaves says that there were sixty-one wagons and one carriage. We have assumed that the number is about seventy since this is the number chosen by Oliva in his careful examination of the incident at Johnson's Ranch (Leo Oliva, "Chivington and the Mules at Johnson's Ranch," *Wagon Tracks—The Santa Fe Trail Association Quarterly* 6, no. 4 [August 1992]).

14. For detailed specification of numbers of soldiers, refer to discussion in Appendix. Hall, *Confederate Army.* Since Scurry lists his companies and does not mention the two companies from the Second (those commanded by Jett and Stafford), we have assumed that they were detailed elsewhere on the twenty-eighth, perhaps back to Santa Fe.

15. See Chapter 5, note 2.

16. See Hall (*Confederate Army,* various entries) for biographical information on the Texan officers. See *Overton Sharp-Shooter,* February 23, 1888, for the commanders when Scurry left Johnson's Ranch.

17. *Overton Sharp-Shooter,* February 23, 1888.

18. Scurry's description of his initial deployment clearly suggests that his outriders were not detected by the Union forces (Scurry to Jackson, March 31, 1862, OR, I: 9, 542–44).

19. Alberts, *Rebels,* 78–79.

20. Scurry to Jackson, March 31, 1862, OR, I: 9, 542–44; note that Davidson reports Scurry in the center and Raguet on the left (*Overton Sharp-Shooter,* March 1, 1888), but Scurry's report is considered more reliable.

21. *Overton Sharp-Shooter,* March 1, 1888.

22. This description of Pigeon's Ranch is based on a line drawing by Vincent Colyer in the Museum of Albuquerque ("Pigeon's Ranch—famous stopping place en route to Santa Fe from Fort Bascom," Vincent Colyer, May 1869, Museum of Albuquerque accession number 85.30.5), the closest picture (in time) to the date of the battle. This drawing was made looking to the west from a point several hundred yards down the Santa Fe Trail. A hint of the south-facing facade of the ranch house can also be seen in a pencil sketch by battle participant John Dare Howland (Nolie Mumey, *The Art and Activities of John Dare Howland* [Boulder: Johnson Press, 1973]).

23. Enos to McFiman, April 5, 1862.

24. The use of Chapin in place of Howland is puzzling. There are several possible reasons. Slough could have felt that because of the terrain and foliage, cavalry would not be particularly helpful (a sentiment echoed by others as well) and so have chosen an infantry commander to lead dismounted troopers. He might not have anticipated any action and so kept Howland back as an advisor, recognizing that he [Slough] had no battle experience and that Howland, a regular army veteran, was fresh from Valverde. He may have recalled Canby's orders to "keep the regular cavalry in reserve" or, finally, he might have kept Howland back as something of a rebuke for his alleged poor performance at Apache Canyon (suggested in Whitford, *Colorado Volunteers*, 89).

25. Heyman, *Prudent Soldier*, 183n. 69.

26. *Overton Sharp-Shooter*, March 1, 1888, describes the shouting incident and notes that Scurry's advance guard included men from the Brigands.

27. Alberts, *Rebels*, 79.

28. *Rocky Mountain News* 4, no. 7, "The Battle of Pigeon's Ranch," June 7, 1862. (Note that, although only the byline "Union" is given, this article was apparently written by Captain Jacob Downing, the commanding officer of Company D of the First Colorado; although later in the article, it is stated that he denied that he was this "Union.")

29. Tappan to Chapin, May 21, 1862, OR, I: 9, 536–38; Ritter to Chapin, May 16, 1862, OR, I: 9, 539–49; *Rocky Mountain Herald*, May 1, 1862. The *Rocky Mountain News* (June 7, 1862) describes both the deployment and Slough's demeanor.

30. Walker to Macrae, May 20, 1862, OR, I: 9, 531–32; *Rocky Mountain News*, June 7, 1862.

31. Scurry to Jackson, March 31, 1862, OR, I: 9, 542–44. *Overton Sharp-Shooter*, March 8, 1888.

32. *Overton Sharp-Shooter*, March 8, 1888.

33. See Appendix for detailed listing of casualties; Peticolas says that there were five prisoners taken during this fight (Alberts, *Rebels*, 79); Tappan (Tappan to Chapin, May 21, 1862, OR, I: 9,

536–38) notes that Company I held its position for about one-half hour. The phrase "to see the elephant" was used by Civil War veterans to describe the reality of battle as distinguished from the romantic visions held by some unbloodied recruits and volunteers. It originated with the tent shows and circuses of the time when one had to pay to get inside to "see the elephant."

34. Tappan to Chapin, May 21, 1862, OR, I: 9, 536–38; also *Rocky Mountain News*, June 7, 1862.

35. Hollister, *Colorado Volunteers*, 69.

36. *Rocky Mountain News*, June 7, 1862. Note that Downing almost certainly made the common mistake of referring to canister as grape, the latter being used almost exclusively in naval guns.

37. *Rocky Mountain News*, June 7, 1862.

38. Ritter's movements and the results of his artillery work during the forenoon are described in Ritter to Chapin, May 16, 1862, OR, I: 9, 539–40 and by Tappan (Tappan to Chapin, March 28, 1862, OR, I: 9, 536–38).

39. Scurry to Jackson, March 31, 1862, OR, I: 9, 542–44 and Alberts, *Rebels*, 79.

Chapter 7

1. Tappan to Chapin, May 21, OR, I: 9, 536; *Rocky Mountain News*, June 7, 1862.

2. *Rocky Mountain News*, June 7, 1862; Hollister, *Colorado Volunteers*, 111–12; Walker to Macrae, May 20, 1862, OR, I: 9, 532.

3. Hollister, *Colorado Volunteers*, 114.

4. Scurry to Jackson, March 31, 1862, OR, I: 9, 543.

5. Tappan to Chapin, May 21, 1862, OR, I: 9, 537.

6. Claflin wrote that he thought the enemy was preparing to charge his battery, and he moved to join Ritter when Captain Chapin "advised" him to do so (Claflin to Chapin, May 18, 1862, in "Claims Considered under the Act of July 4, 1864 and Rejected—1875–1895," NA, RG92, files of the Quartermaster General, Box 148, package 49; Tappan to Chapin, May 21, 1862, OR, I: 9, 537).

7. According to Downing, part of Company D

moved to the right flank of its own volition, Slough being so far to the rear that no orders could be obtained from him (*Rocky Mountain News*, June 7, 1862).

8. Subsequent to the promotion of Shropshire to major, Private Steven Monroe Wells was elected captain of Company A of the Fifth. Due to the capture of Wells at Apache Canyon and the absence of Lieutenants Wright and Oakes, command of Company A had devolved to Sergeant Carson (Hall, *Confederate Army,* 149; *Overton Sharp-Shooter*, March 8, 1888).

9. *Overton Sharp-Shooter*, March 8, 1888.

10. Whitford, *Colorado Volunteers,* 110; J. M. Carson, letter to Mrs. E. G. Gordon, May 31, 1920; *Overton Sharp-Shooter*, March 8, 1888.

11. Buckholts's death is noted by Noel (*A Campaign,* 24). Shannon was exchanged for Captain Charles B. Stivers, Seventh U.S. Infantry, and promoted to major, effective the date of the Battle of Glorieta Pass. (Hall, *Confederate Army,* 160) The account of Shannon's capture used here is taken from Tappan's official report. (Tappan to Chapin, May 21, 1862, OR, I: 9, 537). Another account (*Overton Sharp-Shooter*, February 23, 1888) has it that Shannon was captured while pursuing the Federals subsequent to their final stand.

12. Alberts, *Rebels,* 82.

13. The identification of the Federal officer who spoke to Peticolas as Lieutenant Colonel Tappan is an inference. In fact Peticolas said that the man was a major. Since there were no Federal majors on the field, since the insignia for the two ranks are similar, and since Peticolas's description—dark eyes, whiskers, rather handsome—fits, Tappan would seem to be a good bet. If the officer was indeed Tappan, he may have eventually caught on, inasmuch as he reported that he had been approached by some Texans dressed in the uniform of Colorado Volunteers and that he had at first held his fire, thinking the party might be part of Chivington's command (Tappan to Chapin, May 21, 1862, OR, I: 9, 537).

14. Peticolas reported three occasions on which

he had been mistaken for a Colorado Volunteer (Alberts, *Rebels,* 82–83).

15. *Rocky Mountain News*, June 7, 1862.

16. Ritter to Chapin, May 16, 1862, OR, I: 9, 540.

17. *Rocky Mountain News*, June 7, 1862.

18. Ritter to Chapin, May 16, 1862, OR, I: 9, 540.

19. In a letter to his brother, Tappan reported that "Lieutenant Chambers is maimed for life—one leg is much shorter than the other and his shoulder will trouble him as long as he lives." (Tappan diary—microfilm copy courtesy Charles Meketa); Claflin to Chapin, May 18, 1862; *Rocky Mountain News*, June 7, 1862.

20. Tappan probably followed a route on the south side of the pass close to that taken by the railroad today. Claflin to Chapin, May 18, 1862; Tappan to Chapin, May 21, 1862, OR, I: 9, 537.

21. Enos to McFiman, April 5, 1862.

22. Scurry's account of the final phase of the battle states that the Federal artillery escaped while the infantry was engaged in close combat with the Texans. At that point the infantry broke ranks and fled precipitously, cutting loose their teams and setting fire to two of their wagons (Scurry to Jackson, March 31, 1862, OR, I: 9, 544). In an amusing rejoinder, the *Santa Fe Gazette* (April 6, 1862) reported that "one or two [Federal wagons] became disabled and in the excitement of the moment were set on fire. From this trivial circumstance it seems that the enemy concluded Col. Slough had abandoned the field and given up the day." Enos to McFiman, April 5, 1862; Scurry to Jackson, March 31, 1862, OR, I: 9, 544. Note that Enos implies that all the wagons were saved.

23. Ritter to Chapin, May 16, 1862, OR, I: 9, 540; Hollister, *Colorado Volunteers,* 115; Enos to McFiman, March 29, 1862.

24. David B. Gracy, II, ed., "New Mexico Campaign Letters of Frank Starr," *Military History of Texas and the Southwest* 4, no. 3 (Fall 1964): 177–78.

25. Whitford, *Colorado Volunteers,* 112–14.

26. Tappan to Chapin, May 21, 1862, OR, I: 9, 537; Gracy, *Starr Letters,* 178.

27. *Rocky Mountain News*, June 7, 1862.

28. *Rocky Mountain News*, May 1, 1862.

29. Hollister, *Colorado Volunteers*, 112. Note that Hollister was mistaken about Walker—his company had led the first skirmishers of the morning.

30. Canby to Slough, March 18, 1862, OR, I: 9, 649.

31. Farmer, J. E. Farmer Manuscript, 45–46. The accusation against Lord, if it occurred at all, seems to have been informal since his September Court of Inquiry did not mention any alleged misconduct at Glorieta (Record of Lord Court of Inquiry).

32. About 40 of the 150 troopers had been assigned as a rear guard with Chivington under the command of Lieutenant John Falvey.

Chapter 8

1. Chivington to AG, March 28, 1862, OR, I: 9, 538–39. Chivington refers to the Federal encampment as Camp Lewis; Slough notes it as Kozlowski's Ranch. Sunrise on March 28 was about 6:00 AM.

2. Hollister, *Colorado Volunteers*, 116.

3. Slough to AG, March 30, 1862, OR, I: 9, 533–34. In fact Scurry and the Texans had anticipated an attack on Johnson's Ranch on the twenty-seventh; but when none came they moved forward into the pass on the morning of the twenty-eighth (Westphall, *Glorieta Pass*, 147).

4. The details of Chivington's command are specified in the Appendix—this number includes officers as well as Falvey's forty cavalrymen.

5. Biographical information on Samuel Logan from his obituary in the *Denver Tribune*, August 7, 1883. The supplement to the March post return for Fort Union shows Company G of the Fourth New Mexico Volunteers assigned to Captain James Ford. Company G appears to have been a temporary reassignment of men from the other companies of the Fourth New Mexico to support Slough's battalion, since it does not appear on the Fort Union returns before March 1862 and it is gone after May 1862. It is noted as having eighty-three men and three officers on the May return, and we believe that on March 28, 1862, the company may have been divided with part of the group accompanying Ford and the rest supporting the "seventy-man police guard" at Pigeon's Ranch referred to by Tappan (Tappan to Chapin, May 21, 1862, OR, I: 9, 536). This is qualitatively supported in Whitford (*Colorado Volunteers*, 101) where it is stated that the force that marched to Pigeon's Ranch included "a broken company of New Mexican volunteers."

6. Chivington to AG, March 28, 1862, OR, I: 9, 538–39, footnote.

7. *March of the First*, 10.

8. Chivington to AG, March 28, 1862, OR, I: 9, 538–39.

9. Marc Simmons, *Little Lion of the Southwest* (Albuquerque: University of New Mexico Press, 1973). Chacon also confirms Chaves's participation (Meketa, *Legacy of Honor*, 183).

10. There are few viable access points to the top of Glorieta Mesa on its north and east faces. Although the specific route that Chivington took on the morning of March 28 is not specified, it seems most likely that the battalion moved west, roughly along the present-day course of the railroad and Interstate 25. At the mouth of San Cristobal canyon, the group turned southwest for about one and one-half miles and climbed up the draw to the point where it passes between two 7,800-foot prominences (Note—San Cristobal Canyon is mentioned by Whitford [*Colorado Volunteers*, 116] but not shown by name on the current topographic map). From here the group probably turned west, following the 7,500-foot contour for about three miles. At this point they probably moved through a relatively narrow "corridor" between two steeper sections onto the anvil-shaped area that overlooks Johnson's Ranch to the northeast. This evaluation (and the one in note 40 of this chapter regarding the return march) are speculative and are based on an evaluation of two U.S. Geological Service 7.5 minute quadrangle maps—Pecos, NM and Glorieta, NM.

11. Chivington does not report this move.

Whitford suggests that the scout actually went back toward Pigeon's Ranch (*Colorado Volunteers,* 116) because "they heard the discharge of artillery at Pigeon's Ranch." Hollister (*Colorado Volunteers,* 110) says that the scout (under a "Lt. Falvia") went south toward Galisteo. We are inclined to favor the Hollister account since the time at which the troops turned off the Galisteo road would have preceded the opening of hostilities at Pigeon's Ranch by thirty minutes to one hour. Biographical information on Falvey from Thomas H. S. Hamersley, ed., *Complete Regular Army Register of the United States for One Hundred Years* (1779–1879) (Washington, D.C.: Thomas H. S. Hamersley, 1888), 433.

12. Whitford (*Colorado Volunteers,* 116) noted that Chivington's battalion heard cannon fire from Pigeon's Ranch, although he suggests it was before the cavalrymen turned south. Given the distance from Pigeon's Ranch (approximately five miles), it is certainly credible that the sound would have carried to the top of the mesa. In his occasionally faulty memoirs, Chivington also reported that he "heard the battle open" from the bluff (Martin H. Hall, "John M. Chivington," *New Mexico Historical Review* 33, no. 2 [April 1958]: 144–55).

13. Whitford, *Colorado Volunteers,* 116.

14. Ibid.

15. See appendix for details of Confederate numbers and casualties at Johnson's Ranch.

16. In fact Chivington was later accused of a level of caution that bordered on cowardice (Waldrip, *New Mexico During the Civil War,* 266 citing *Rio Abajo Weekly Press,* March 8, 1864). Waldrip suggests that it took Lewis two hours to persuade Chivington to proceed with the attack. Chivington wrote that they arrived at the overlook between 1:30 and 2:00 P.M. (Chivington to AG, March 28, 1862, OR, I: 9, 538–39) so the actual start of the descent could have been as late as 3:30 P.M.

17. Whitford, *Colorado Volunteers,* 118. The authors personally climbed and descended the slope and can attest to its steepness as well as the time required.

18. The cited newspaper article suggests that Lewis, not Chivington, should get full credit for the overrun of the Confederate train at Johnson's Ranch. See note 28 below.

19. P. D. Browne, "Captain T. D. Nettles and the Valverde Battery," *Texana* 2, no. 1 (Spring 1964): 1–2.

20. Davidson says that Nettles actually spiked the cannon then torched off the caisson which "burnt him all over" (*Overton Sharp-Shooter,* March 1, 1888). Whitford (*Colorado Volunteers,* 119) says that Lewis and Sanford spiked the piece. The *Santa Fe Gazette* (April 26, 1862) says Lewis spiked cannon.

21. In his official report, Chivington claimed to have killed twenty-seven, wounded sixty-three, and captured seventeen (Chivington to AG, March 28, 1862, OR, I: 9, 538–39). A careful review of Confederate records suggests that better numbers are as cited (Hall, *Confederate Army*). Some of the sixty-three wounded may have been injured in earlier action at Apache Canyon on the twenty-sixth and were under treatment at the field hospital at Johnson's Ranch.

22. *Overton Sharp-Shooter,* March 1, 1888.

23. Scurry to Jackson, March 31, 1862, OR, I: 9, 542–44. For a discussion of Chivington and Sand Creek see Clark, *Fighting Parson,* especially 244–60.

24. Bloom, *Confederate Reminiscences,* 319. Note that if Lewis was in command on the scene, he, rather than Chivington, probably should bear the brunt of this criticism.

25. Whitford, *Colorado Volunteers,* 122.

26. Chivington, "The First Colorado."

27. The controversy over who should receive credit for the successful destruction of the Confederate train bubbled throughout New Mexico for almost two years. Collins, publisher of the *Santa Fe Gazette,* claimed that he was in charge of burning the train (*Santa Fe Gazette,* April 24, 1862), a claim Chivington specifically refutes in a postscript to his official report (Chivington to AG, March 28, 1862, OR, I: 9, 538–39). Meanwhile the *Rio Abajo Press,* and eventually even the Terri-

torial Legislature, said that Lewis and not Chivington should get the credit (*Rio Abajo Press*, March 8, 1864 and New Mexico Territorial legislature resolution dated January 23, 1864) noting that ". . . we object to Colonel Chivington's strutting about in plumage stolen from Captain William H. [sic] Lewis, Fifth US Infantry." Whitford, *Colorado Volunteers*, 120.

28. Chivington, "The First Colorado;" J. M. Chivington, "The Pet Lambs," *Denver Republican*, April 20, 1890.

29. Ed. *Civil War Times Illustrated*, "The Pet Lambs at Glorieta Pass," 34. *March of the First*, 12–13.

30. Oliva, *Chivington and the Mules*.

31. Whitford, *Colorado Volunteers*, 120–22.

32. Ed. *Civil War Times Illustrated*, "The Pet Lambs at Glorieta Pass," 34, and Chivington to AG, March 28, 1862, OR, I: 9, 538–39. If the messenger had been dispatched from Pigeon's Ranch at about the time of Slough's second retreat (after 3:00 P.M.), he would have arrived at the overlook location at about 5:30 P.M., approximately the time at which Chivington's men would have begun to reassemble at the top of the mesa.

33. Sunset on March 28 was at about 6:30 P.M.

34. We hypothesize that Cobb was the second messenger and that he was dispatched in the late afternoon since Whitford (*Colorado Volunteers*, 122) says that a lieutenant gave the order to return to Kozlowski's Ranch and since it seems more likely that Slough would send an officer if his intent was to countermand a previous order.

35. Chivington, "The First Colorado."

36. It is plausible that Grzelachowski accompanied Cobb with the express intent of guiding the column back to Kozlowski's Ranch. Francis Kajencki, "Alexander Grzelachowski—Pioneer Merchant of Puerto Luna, New Mexico," *Arizona and the West* 2 (Autumn 1984): 243–60, and Francis Kajencki, "The Battle of Glorieta Pass: Was the Guide Ortiz or Grzelachowski?" *New Mexico Historical Review* 62, no. 1 (January 1987): 47–54.

37. It seems plausible that the ex-priest would

have led the Coloradans south to Padre Spring Creek. They probably followed the creek bed roughly northeast to a steep (albeit much less so than all of the other options!) draw about one mile west-northwest of Cerro de Escobas where they descended to the valley bottom about three and one-half miles west of Kozlowski's Ranch.

38. One of the strongest pieces of evidence for Grzelachowski's participation is his request for compensation for the death of his horse and the government's accedence (Grzelachowski to Chapin with endorsement, August 4, 1862, Letters Received, Department of New Mexico, 1854–1865, NA, RG94).

39. *March of the First*, 13.

40. Hollister, *Colorado Volunteers*, 117.

Chapter 9

1. Bloom, *Confederate Reminiscences*, 317–18.

2. Although both Peticolas and Davidson suggested that Pyron was the truce bearer (Alberts, *Rebels*, 86; *Overton Sharp-Shooter*, March 1, 1888), it does not seem reasonable for Scurry to have sent his senior battlefield commander. The reference to Jackson in Whitford (*Colorado Volunteers*, 115) seems more credible. Scurry does not specifically identify the truce bearer.

3. Downing letter to *Rocky Mountain News*, n.d., 3, noted as from MSS, XI–20, Colorado Historical Society.

4. Noel, *A Campaign*, 23 and Davidson (*Overton Sharp-Shooter*, March 1, 1888) refer to snow "near a foot deep" on the evening of the twenty-eighth.

5. Slough to AG, March 30, 1862, OR, I: 9, 535; Alberts, *Rebels*, 86; *Overton Sharp-Shooter*, March 1, 1888.

6. *Overton Sharp-Shooter*, March 1, 1888.

7. Mamie Yeary, *Reminiscences of the Boys in Grey* (1912; repr. Dayton: Morningside Press, 1986), 760–61.

8. Shannon spent much of his Confederate career in captivity, although this was not particu-

larly detrimental to his personal advancement in rank. He was promoted to major during his post-Glorieta captivity. After being exchanged following Glorieta, he was captured again at Fort Butler in June 1863 and remained in captivity until March 1865. While in this period of captivity, he was promoted to lieutenant colonel (Dwight to Szymanski, November 1, 1864, OR, II: 7, 1077–78; Christensen to Hitchcock, December 16, 1864, OR, II: 7, 1232–23; Canby's endorsement on Dwight to Christensen, OR, II: 8, 142; Hoffman to Hill, February 15, 1865, OR, II: 8, 229; Dwight to Szymanski, March 15, 1865, OR, II: 8, 402–3; Szymanski to Dwight, March 25, 1865, OR, II: 8, 430–31; Shannon service record, NA, RG109).

9. Scurry to Sibley, March 30, 1862, OR, I: 9, 541; *Overton Sharp-Shooter*, February 23, 1888.

10. Scurry to Sibley, March 30, 1862, OR, I: 9, 541.

11. *Santa Fe Gazette*, April 26, 1862.

12. Ochiltree to Davis, April 27, 1862, *Official Reports of Battles as Published by the Order of the Confederate Congress at Richmond* (New York, 1863). Biographical information on Ochiltree from Hall, *Planter vs. Frontiersman*, 59–60.

13. Giese, *Echoes*, 12.

14. Slough to AG, March 30, 1862, OR, I: 9, 534–36.

15. Whitford, *Colorado Volunteers*, 115.

16. Scurry to Sibley, March 30, 1862, OR, I: 9, 541–42.

17. *Overton Sharp-Shooter*, March 1, 1888.

18. Bloom, *Confederate Reminiscences*, 318.

19. Bloom, *Confederate Reminiscences*, 320; *Overton Sharp-Shooter*, March 15, 1888; Heyman, *Prudent Soldier*, 183.

20. *Santa Fe Gazette* resolution, May 31, 1862.

21. Slough to AG, March 30, 1862, OR, I: 9, 534–36.

22. Hollister, *Colorado Volunteers*, 121. The specifics of Canby's orders are unknown. The reports are secondhand with Slough as the source, hence there is room for doubt regarding their accuracy. It is also interesting to note that both Hollister (*Colorado Volunteers*, 121) and Connelly

(Connelly to Seward, April 6, 1862, OR, I: 9, 660) stated that the orders were personally delivered by Canby's adjutant, Captain William J. L. Nicodemus, yet there is a letter in the Official Records written by Nicodemus at Fort Craig on the same day that he was said to have delivered the message to Slough at Bernal Springs, four or five days north of Fort Craig (Nicodemus to Carson, March 31, 1862, OR, I: 9, 659).

23. *Rocky Mountain News*, June 7, 1862.

24. Arthur A. Wright, "Colonel John P. Slough and the New Mexico Campaign," *The Colorado Magazine* 39 (April 1962): 82–88.

25. Letter from Tappan to Chivington dated January 23, 1863, in *Diary and Letters of Samuel F. Tappan* (microfilm copy courtesy Charles Meketa).

26. Faulkner, "With Sibley in New Mexico," 140.

27. Thompson, *Westward the Texans*, 96.

28. It is interesting to note that Scurry asked Sibley for ammunition for his artillery, but nothing else (Scurry to Sibley, March 30, 1862, OR, I: 9, 541).

29. It is hard to tell from Sibley's report to Richmond whether he considered himself better or worse off as a result of the Battle of Glorieta Pass or what he might do next (Sibley to Cooper, March 30, 1862, OR, I: 9, 541).

30. Thompson, *Westward the Texans*, 20.

31. Faulkner, "With Sibley in New Mexico," 140.

32. Sibley to Cooper, May 4, 1862, OR, I: 9, 509; Some of the "confiscation" may have taken place at Pigeon's Ranch (see Alexander Valle claim records, op. cit.).

33. Letter from Collins to Dole, April 26, 1862 (NA, RG75); *Santa Fe Gazette*, April 26, 1862; Hall, *Sibley's New Mexico Campaign*, 166.

34. Sibley to Cooper, May 4, 1862, OR, I: 9, 510.

35. Canby to AG, April 23, 1862, OR, I: 9, 550–51.

36. Chacon briefly describes the "Battle of Albuquerque" (Meketa, *Legacy of Honor*, 183–85).

37. Brown, *Pioneers*, 398.

38. Don Alberts, "The Battle of Peralta," *New Mexico Historical Review* 58, no. 4 (October 1983): 369–79.

39. Graydon to Paul, May 14, 1862, OR, I: 9, 671–72; Jerry Thompson, *Desert Tiger: Captain Paddy Graydon and the Civil War in the Far Southwest* (El Paso: Texas Western Press, 1992), 44–46.

40. Alberts, *Rebels*, 112.

Chapter 10

1. *Overton Sharp-Shooter*, October 13, 1887.
2. Hall, *Planter vs Frontiersman*, 62.
3. Teel, *Sibley's New Mexico Campaign*.
4. Finch, *A Confederate Pathway*, 88.
5. *Overton Sharp-Shooter*, October 13, 1887.
6. Sibley to Cooper, April 4, 1862, OR, I: 9, 512.
7. Thompson, *Westward the Texans*, 19.
8. Roberts, *Death Comes for the Chief Justice;* Marion Dargon, "New Mexico's Fight for Statehood," *New Mexico Historical Review* 15, no. 2 (April 1940): 133–87; Arie Poldervaart, "Black-Robed Justice in New Mexico, 1846–1912," *New Mexico Historical Review* 22, no. 2 (April 1947): 109–39; and 22, no. 3 (July 1947): 286–314.
9. Craig, *Fighting Parson*.
10. Kansas Historical Collection, Vol. 13, 1913–1914, 71–79.
11. *Denver Post*, January 19, 1913; *Trail Magazine* 5, no. 9 (February 1913), 28.
12. *The Friday Evening Times*, Denver, Colorado, March 3, 1905, 1; Alvin T. Steinel, *History of Agriculture in Colorado* (Fort Collins: State Agricultural College, 1926), 411–15. Note that Downing actually got the alfalfa seeds during a visit to El Paso while he was stationed in southern New Mexico.
13. Thompson, *Henry Hopkins Sibley;* Walter B. Hesseltine and Hazel C. Wolf, *The Blue and Grey on the Nile* (Chicago: University of Chicago Press, 1961), 113–14.
14. Warner, *Generals in Grey*, 270–71.
15. *Encyclopedia of Texas*, Vol. 3, 1906.
16. Finch, *A Confederate Pathway*, 173.
17. Alberts, *Rebels*.
18. L. E. Daniell, *Texas: The Country and its Men*, 534–35.

19. Douglas W. Owsley, *Bioarcheology on a Battlefield: The Abortive Confederate Campaign in New Mexico*, Museum of New Mexico, Office of Archeological Studies, Archeology Notes 142, 1994, 42.
20. Whitford, *Colorado Volunteers*, 125.
21. *Albuquerque Tribune*, November 7, 1988.
22. This is reported in "Consolidated Forensic Data," an attachment to an undated news release from the Museum of New Mexico news service, obtained at the reburial ceremony.
23. Owsley, *Bioarcheology*, 45–48.

Appendix

1. Chivington to AG, March 26, 1862, OR, I: 9, 538–39.
2. See Chapter 4, note 8.
3. Federal casualties from Apache Canyon are taken from Whitford (Colorado Volunteers) or the *Colorado Republican* and *Rocky Mountain News*, May 1, 1862 unless otherwise noted.
4. Hollister, *Colorado Volunteers*, 107.
5. Chivington says that there were fourteen wounded and Hollister says thirteen. Only eleven names have been confirmed.
6. *Overton Sharp-Shooter*, February 23, 1888; Oscar Haas, trans., "The Diary of Julius Giesecke, 1861–1862," *Texas Military History* 3, no. 4 (Winter, 1963), 237; Hall, "Journal of Ebeneezer Hanna," 28; Haas, "Eggeling, Hoffman Letters;" Thompson, *Westward the Texans*, 96; McCown, "Letter to the Bellville Countryman;" McLeary, *A Comprehensive History*, 700; Alberts, *Rebels*, 76; O'Donnell, *The Diary of Robert Thomas Williams*, 8; Walker to Macrae, May 20, 1862, OR, I: 9, 531; *Santa Fe Gazette*, April 26, 1862.
7. *Santa Fe Gazette*, April 26, 1862.
8. Ibid.
9. All information is based on Hall (Confederate Army) unless otherwise noted.
10. Noel lists T. H. Harris as killed at Glorieta. Hall notes that one Travis Washington Harris, age 18, died on March 26 but makes no mention of

the death being battle related (Noel, *A Campaign,* 131; Hall, *Confederate Army,* 71).

11. Private Tate was assigned to company D of the 2nd Texas which was in Albuquerque on March twenty-sixth. We have assumed that he was temporarily detailed to Pyron's Apache Canyon command and have arbitrarily assigned him to Company E.

12. Davidson notes that Terrell's wound was mortal and that Tooke, McLeary, and Tinkler were captured (*Overton Sharp-Shooter,* February 23, 1888).

13. Although the men whose names are shown with asterisks may have been captured on March 28, it seems more likely that they were taken prisoner on March 26 so they are totaled in the casualty records for that day.

14. Hall (Confederate Army, 164) says that Sullock may have been taken prisoner March 2 [sic], 1862 at Apache Canyon.

15. Hanna (Hall, "Journal of Ebeneezer Hanna") says that there were six Confederate wounded; and Williams (O'Donnell, 8) says five although Hall lists only one (Sapp).

16. Both Chivington (Chivington to AG, March 26, 1862, OR, I: 9, 530–31) and the anonymous author of the "March of the First" (*March of the First,* 9) allege that the Coloradans captured more prisoners at Apache Canyon than we can account for by name. Chivington says seventy-one and the March of the First says sixty-five. Although Hall (*Confederate Army*) is quite specific, we assume that Chivington should have known so we use seventy-one as the correct number.

17. Strictly speaking, Company F of the First Colorado was not under the direct command of Tappan, at least until later in the battle. In addition Tappan did direct the artillery early in the battle. These niceties are reflected on the order of battle figure.

18. If Chivington had 297 of the 916 First Colorado total, this leaves 619 with Slough.

19. Chivington to AG, March 28, 1862, OR, I: 9, 538.

20. Ibid.

21. Slough to AG, March 30, 1862, OR, I: 9, 534.

22. Ibid.

23. See Chapter 6, note 10.

24. From Whitford, *Colorado Volunteers; March of the First,* 36; *Colorado Republican* and *Rocky Mountain Herald,* May 1, 1862; Hollister, *Colorado Volunteers; Rocky Mountain.News,* May 31, 1862; unless otherwise noted.

25. These men were all listed as "missing" in articles in the *Colorado Republican* and *Rocky Mountain Herald,* May 1, 1862. They are assumed to have been captured and exchanged because their individual service records in the National Archives confirm that they served out their terms and were not killed or wounded. The same articles also list two additional men, H. S. Hillman and George Weaghly, but no service records were found for these individuals so they are not listed in this compilation.

26. These four men are all included in the list of wounded in "March of the First." Since Company E went with Chivington to Johnson's Ranch and since these casualties occurred at Pigeon's Ranch, it is assumed that some men from Company E remained at Pigeon's Ranch on the 28th.

27. Ford and Osborn were confirmed by service record verification.

28. There is a specific entry in Bacus's service record which states "taken prisoner in Battle of Pejus Ranche [sic] March 28—released on parole April 1."

29. *Rocky Mountain News,* May 31, 1862 says the man's name was Henry.

30. Alberts, *Rebels,* 79.

31. Both Denison and Percival have service records which show that they served well beyond the New Mexico campaign. There is a specific entry in Denison's service record which states "taken prisoner at Apache Canyon March 28, 1862."

32. Claflin's letter (Claflin to Chapin, May 18, 1862) reports these two deserters.

33. The artillery batteries were staffed by men from the Fifth U.S. Infantry and the First and Second U.S. Cavalry. The post return for Fort

Union notes that the Federal artillery was made up of the Fifth U.S. Infantry. A process of elimination implies that it was 5/E since 5/A and 5/G were at Johnson's Ranch. Ritter to Chapin, May 16, 1862, OR, I: 9, 539–40; *Colorado Republican* and *Rocky Mountain Herald*; War Department casualty list dated March 14, 1867.

34. Post return for 3rd U.S. cavalry (NA, RG94).

35. Sibley to Cooper, March 31, 1862, OR, I: 9, 540–41.

36. Scurry to Jackson, March 31, 1862, OR, I: 9, 542–45.

37. McLeary, *A Comprehensive History,* 700.

38. Bloom, *Confederate Reminiscences,* Holcomb letter; Haas, "Eggeling, Hoffmann Letters."

39. Hall, *Confederate Army.*

40. *Overton Sharp-Shooter,* February 23, 1888.

41. Meketa, *Legacy of Honor,* 188–89.

42. Apache Canyon numbers reduced by casualties.

43. Ibid.

44. Information from Hall (*Confederate Army*) unless otherwise noted.

45. O'Donnell, *The Diary of Robert Thomas Williams.*

46. Noel (*A Campaign,* 131) also lists one F. Jasper, but Hall shows no person by such a name in the Sibley Brigade.

47. Noel (*A Campaign,* 124) states that William Ramsey was wounded at Glorieta, but Hall has no such notation.

48. Howell (Thompson, *Westward the Texans,* 96) notes that Cabeen and Dubose were wounded and captured on the twenty-eighth, not the twenty-sixth.

49. Union order of battle comes from Whitford, *Colorado Volunteers,* 115–16; also Chivington to AG, March 28, 1862, OR, I: 9, 538–39.

50. See Chapter 8, note 5.

51. 5th U.S. Infantry regimental returns (NA RG94); list of casualties dated March 14, 1867.

52. Scurry to Jackson, March 31, 1862, OR, I: 9, 542–45.

53. Whitford, *Colorado Volunteers,* 119.

54. McLeary, *Comprehensive History,* 700.

55. Chivington to AG, March 28, 1862, OR, I: 9, 538–39.

56. Since Company B is not listed by Scurry as accompanying him to Pigeon's Ranch, we have assumed that B was probably elsewhere, perhaps in Santa Fe, on March 28. It seems most likely that Cavillo was captured at Johnson's Ranch.

57. Davidson (*Overton Sharp-Shooter,* March 1, 1888) reports that Nettles was "burnt all over" when a limber box exploded after he spiked the cannon.

Bibliography

Manuscript Sources

F. R. Collard
Colorado State Historical Society
    Biographical Files
    Manuscript File
    Newsclipping File
Harold B. Simpson Confederate Research Center, Hill College, Hillsboro, Texas
National Archives of the United States
    Record Group 59: Territorial Papers of the U.S. Department of State
    Record Group 75: Letters Received by the Office of Indian Affairs
    Record Group 92: Quartermaster General, Consolidated File
    Record Group 94: post returns, letters sent, letters rec'd, regimental returns (1 Cav, 3 Cav, 5th Inf)
    Record Group 94: Compiled Service Records of the New Mexico Volunteers
    Record Group 94: Listing of Service Records of the Colorado Volunteers
    Record Group 109: Compiled Service Records of Confederate Soldiers
    Record Group 393: Letters Sent, Department of New Mexico
Rodgers Library, New Mexico Highlands University, Las Vegas, New Mexico
Ruhlen Collection, New Mexico State University
Texas State Library

Government Documents

General Services Administration—National Archives and Record Service. *Military Operations of the Civil War.* Vol. 4. 1980.
Gideon, J. S. *Cavalry Tactics—First Part.* Washington, D.C.: U.S. War Department, 1841.
National Park Service. "Fort Union National Monument, New Mexico: General Management Plan." Santa Fe: National Park Service, 1985.
Official Reports of Battles as Published by the Order of the Confederate Congress at Richmond. New York, 1863.
Proceedings of a Court of Inquiry in the Case of Captain R. S. C. Lord, First U.S. Cavalry by Headquarters, Department of New Mexico under Special Order No. 171. September 22, 1862.
Strait, Newton A. *An Alphabetical List of Battles: 1754–1900.* U.S. Department of the Interior, Bureau of Pensions, 1905.
United States Army. *Official Army Register of the Volunteer Forces of the United States Army, 1861–1865.* Pt. 8. 1867.
———. Military Division of the Missouri. *Outline Descriptions of the Posts in the Military Division of the Missouri.* Chicago, 1876.
United States Geophysical Survey. 7.5 Minute Topographic Map Series.
    Bull Canyon, New Mexico. N3522.5—W10545/7.5. 1966.

Galisteo, New Mexico. N3522.5—W10552.5/7.5. 1966.

Seton Village, New Mexico. 35-105—E8—TF024. 1993.

Pecos, New Mexico. N3530—W10537.5/7.5. 1961.

Glorieta, New Mexico. 35-105—E7—TF024. 1993.

United States Government Printing Office. *Report of the Joint Committee on the Conduct of the War.* Senate Document No. 108, 37th Congress, 3d sess., Vol. 3, pp. 364–72 (Invasion of New Mexico), 1863.

———. *The War of the Rebellion: A Compilation of the Official Records of the Union and Confederate Armies.* 128 vols. Washington D.C., 1880–1901.

———. *United States Army Regulations of 1861.* Rev. ed. 1863; Yuma: Fort Yuma Press, 1980.

———. "Fort Union National Monument." Informational Brochure published by the National Park Service. 1990.

Utley, Robert M. *Fort Union National Monument, New Mexico.* Washington, D.C.: National Park Service Historical Handbook Series No. 35, 1962.

War Department, Casualty List Dated March 14, 1867.

Diaries and Journals

Alberts, Don, ed. *Rebels on the Rio Grande: The Civil War Journal of A. B. Peticolas.* Albuquerque: University of New Mexico Press, 1984.

Anderson, Hattie M. "With the Confederates in New Mexico—Memoirs of Hank Smith." *Panhandle Plains Historical Review* 2 (1929): 65–97.

Carmony, Neil B., ed. *The Civil War in Apacheland—Sergeant George Hand's Diary.* Silver City: High Lonesome Books, 1996.

J. E. Farmer Diary. Adjutant General Files: New Mexico State Records Center and Archives.

Faulkner, W. A. "With Sibley in New Mexico: The Journal of William Henry Smith." *West Texas Historical Association Yearbook* (October 1951): 111–41.

Giese, Dale F., ed. *My Life with the Army in the West: Memoirs of James E. Farmer, 1858–1898.* Santa Fe: Stagecoach Press, 1993.

Gracy, David B., ed. "New Mexico Campaign Letters of Frank Starr—1861–1862." *Texas Military History* 4 (Fall 1964): 169–88.

Haas, Oscar. "The Diary of Julius Giesecke, 1861–1862." *Texas Military History* 3, no. 4 (Winter 1963): 228–42.

———. "The Diary of Julius Giesecke, 1863–1865." *Texas Military History* 4, no. 1 (Spring 1964): 27–56.

Hanna, Ebenezer. Journal of Ebenezer Hanna. Texas State Archives. Also published by Martin H. Hall in *Password* 3 (January 1958): 14–29.

Hord, Ruth Waldrop. "The Diary of Lieutenant E. L. Robb, CSA, from Santa Fe to Fort Lancaster, 1862." *Permian Historical Annual* 18 (December 1978): 59–80.

O'Donnell, Connie. The Diary of Robert Thomas Williams: Marches, Skirmishes, and Battles of the Fourth Regiment, Texas Militia Volunteers, October 1861–November 1865. Transcribed typescript from the Center for American History, University of Texas.

Mumey, Noel. *Bloody Trails Along the Rio Grande—A Day-by-Day Diary of Alonzo Ferdinand Ickis.* Denver: The Old West Publishing Company, 1958.

Thompson, Jerry D., ed. *Westward the Texans: The Civil War Journal of Private William Randolph Howell.* El Paso: Texas Western Press, 1990.

———. *From Desert to Bayou: The Civil War Journal and Sketches of Morgan Wolfe Merrick.* El Paso: University of Texas at El Paso, 1991.

Newspapers

Albuquerque Tribune
Bellville Countryman
Colorado Republican
Denver Friday Evening Times
Denver Post
Denver Republican
Denver Tribune
National Tribune
New Braunfels Herald
Overton Sharp-Shooter
Rocky Mountain Herald
Rocky Mountain News
Rio Abajo Weekly Press
Santa Fe Gazette

Dissertations and Theses

Jamieson, Perry D. "The Development of Civil War Tactics." Ph.D. Dissertation. Wayne State University, 1979.

Books

Altshuler, Constance Wynn. *Cavalry Yellow and Infantry Blue—Army Officers in Arizona Between 1851 and 1886.* Tucson: Arizona Historical Society, 1995.

Bancroft, Hubert H. *History of Arizona and New Mexico, 1530–1888.* Albuquerque: Horn and Wallace, 1962.

Barr, Alwyn. *Charles Porter's Account of the Confederate Attempt to Seize Arizona and New Mexico.* Austin: Pemberton Press, 1964.

Bowden, J. J. *The Exodus of the Federal Troops from Texas: 1861.* Austin: Eakin Press, 1986.

Brown, John H. *Indian Wars and Pioneers of Texas.* Austin: L. E. Daniell, 1880.

Coates, Earl J., and Dean S. Thomas. *An Introduction to Civil War Small Arms.* Gettysburg: Thomas Publications, 1990.

Colton, Ray C. *The Civil War in the Western Territories.* Norman: University of Oklahoma Press, 1959.

Columbine Genealogical and Historical Society, Inc. *Colorado Territory Civil War Volunteers Records.* Littleton: Columbine Genealogical and Historical Society, Inc., 1994.

Conner, Seymour, and Jimmy Skaggs. *Broadcloth and Britches—The Santa Fe Trade.* College Station: Texas A&M University Press, 1977.

Craig, Reginald. *The Fighting Parson: A Biography of Colonel John M. Chivington.* Los Angeles: Westernlore Press, 1959.

Cullum, George W. *Biographical Register of the Officers and Graduates of the U.S. Military Academy at West Point.* Boston: Houghton, Mifflin, 1891.

Daniell, L. E. *Texas: The Country and its Men.* No publisher or date given (copy obtained from Texas State Archives).

Davis, Elias A., and Edwin H. Grobe. *Encyclopedia of Texas.* Dallas: Texas Development Bureau, n.d.

D'Hamel, E. B. *The Adventures of a Tenderfoot.* Waco: W. M. Morrison, n.d.

Dornbusch, C. E. *Military Bibliography of the Civil War.* Vol. 2. New York: New York Public Library, 1971.

Drury, Ian, and Tony Gibbons. *The Civil War Military Machine.* New York: Smithmark Publishers, 1992.

Ellis, Richard N., ed. *New Mexico Historic Documents.* Albuquerque: University of New Mexico Press, 1975.

Emmett, Chris. *Fort Union and the Winning of the Southwest.* Norman: University of Oklahoma Press, 1965.

Faulk, Odie. *General Tom Green—Fightin' Texan.* Waco: Texian Press, 1963.

Finch, L. Boyd. *Confederate Pathway to the Pacific: Major Sherod Hunter and the Arizona Territory, CSA.* Tucson: Arizona Historical Society, 1996.

Foote, Shelby. *The Civil War.* 3 vols. New York: Vintage Books, 1958.

Frazer, Robert W. *Forts of the West.* Norman: University of Oklahoma Press, 1965.

Frazier, Donald S. *Blood and Treasure—Confederate Empire in the Southwest.* College Station: Texas A&M University Press, 1995.

Fulton, Maurice G., and Paul Horgan. *New Mexico's Own Chronicle.* Dallas: Banks Upshaw, 1937.

Ganaway, Loomis M. *New Mexico and the Sectional Controversy.* Albuquerque: University of New Mexico Press, 1944.

Gregg, Andrew K. *New Mexico in the 19th Century—A Pictorial History.* Albuquerque: University of New Mexico Press, 1968.

———. *Drums of Yesterday: The Forts of New Mexico.* San Francisco: The Press of the Territories, 1968.

Griffith, Paddy. *Battle Tactics of the Civil War.* New Haven: Yale University Press, 1987.

Grinstead, Marion C. *Life and Death of a Frontier Fort: Fort Craig, New Mexico, 1854–1885.* Socorro: Socorro County Historical Society, 1973.

———. *Destiny at Valverde: The Life and Death of Alexander McRae.* Socorro: Socorro County Historical Society, 1992.

Hall, Martin H. *Sibley's New Mexico Campaign.* Austin: University of Texas Press, 1960.

———. *The Confederate Army of New Mexico.* Austin: Presidial Press, 1978.

Hamersley, Thomas H. S. *Complete Regular Army Register of the United States for One Hundred Years (1779–1879).* Washington, D.C.: T. H. S. Hamersley, 1888.

Hardee, Brevet Colonel W. J. *Rifle and Light Infantry Tactics for the Exercise and Maneuvers of Troops when Acting as Light Infantry or Riflemen.* Philadelphia: Lippincott Grambo and Company, 1855.

Harris, Gertrude. *A Tale of Men Who Knew Not Fear.* San Antonio: Alamo Printing Co., 1935.

Hayes, A. A., Jr. *New Colorado and the Santa Fe Trail.* Harper and Brothers, 1880.

Heitman, Francis B. *Historical Record and Dictionary of the United States Army.* U.S. Government Printing Office, 1903; repr. Urbana: University of Illinois Press, 1965.

Hesseltine, William B., and Hazel C. Wolf. *The Blue and Grey on the Nile.* Chicago: University of Chicago Press, 1961.

Heyman, Max. *The Prudent Soldier—A Biography of Major General E. R. S. Canby.* Glendale: Arthur H. Clark Publishers, 1959.

Hollister, Ovando. *Colorado Volunteers in New Mexico, 1842.* Chicago: R. R. Donnelley and Sons, 1962. Also published as *Boldly They Rode.* Lakewood: The Golden Press, 1949.

Horgan, Paul. *Great River.* New York: Rinehart and Company, 1954.

Horn, Calvin. *New Mexico's Troubled Years: The Story of the Early Territorial Governors.* Albuquerque: Horn and Wallace Publishers, 1963.

Horn [Calvin] and [William] Wallace, eds. *Union Army Operations in the Southwest—Final Victory.* Albuquerque: Horn and Wallace, 1961.

———. *Confederate Victories in the Southwest—Prelude to Defeat.* Albuquerque: Horn and Wallace, 1961.

Johnson, Robert U., and Clarence C. Buel, eds. *Battles and Leaders of the Civil War.* Vol. 2. 1883; repr. Secaucus: Castle Press, n.d.

Josephy, Alvin M. Jr., ed. *War on the Frontier—The Trans-Mississippi West* (Richmond: Time-Life Books, 1986).

———. *The Civil War in the American West* (New York: Alfred A. Knopf, 1991).

Journal of the Secession Convention of Texas, 1861. Austin, 1912.

Keleher, W. A. *Turmoil in New Mexico: 1848–1868.* Santa Fe: Rydal Press, 1952.

Kennedy, Francis H., ed. *The Civil War Battlefield Guide.* Boston: Houghton Mifflin Company, 1990.

Kerby, Robert Lee. *The Confederate Invasion of New Mexico and Arizona.* Tucson: Westernlore Press, 1981.

Lewis, Oscar. *The War in the Far West: 1861–1865.* Garden City: Doubleday, 1961.

Lippincott, J. B. *U.S. Infantry Tactics for the Instruction, Exercise, and Maneuvers of the United States Infantry.* Philadelphia: J. B.

Lippincott, 1861.

Mahan, D. H. *An Elementary Treatise on Advanced-Guard, Outpost, and Detachment of Troops.* New York: John Wiley, 1861.

McKee, Major James Cooper. *Narrative of the Surrender of a Command of U.S. Forces at Fort Fillmore, New Mexico, in July, A.D., 1861.* Houston: Stagecoach Press, 1960.

Meketa, Charles and Jacqueline. *One Blanket and Ten Days Rations.* Globe: Southwest Parks and Monument Association, 1980.

Meketa, J. D. *Louis Felsenthal, Citizen Soldier of Territorial New Mexico.* Albuquerque: University of New Mexico Press, 1982.

———, ed. *Legacy of Honor—The Life of Rafael Chacon.* Albuquerque: University of New Mexico Press, 1986.

Miller, Darlis. *The California Column in New Mexico.* Albuquerque: University of New Mexico Press, 1982.

Mills, W. W. *Forty Years at El Paso.* El Paso: Carl Herzog, 1962.

Mumey, Nolie. *The Art and Activities of John Dare Howland.* Boulder: Johnson Publishers, 1973.

Myers, Joan, and Marc Simmons. *Along the Santa Fe Trail.* Albuquerque: University of New Mexico Press, 1986.

Nankivell, Major John H. *History of the Military Organizations of the State of Colorado, 1860–1935.* Denver: W. H. Kistler Stationary Co., 1935.

Noel, Theophilus. *A Campaign from Santa Fe to the Mississippi—Being a History of the Old Sibley Brigade.* 1865; repr. Raleigh, N.C.: Whittet and Shepperson Press, 1961.

Oates, Stephen B. *Confederate Cavalry West of the River.* Austin: University of Texas Press, 1961.

Oliva, Leo E. *Soldiers on the Santa Fe Trail.* Norman: University of Oklahoma Press, 1967.

Raab, James W. *W. W. Loring: Florida's Forgotten General.* Manhattan, KS: Sunflower University Press, 1996.

Richardson, James D. *A Compilation of Messages and Papers of the Confederacy: 1861–1865.* Nashville: United States Publishing Company, 1905.

Roberts, Gary. *Death Comes for the Chief Justice: The Slough-Rynerson Quarrel and Political Violence in New Mexico.* Niwot: University Press of Colorado, 1990.

Sacks, B. *Be It Enacted: The Creation of the Territory of Arizona.* Phoenix: Arizona Historical Foundation, 1964.

Simmons, Marc. *Little Lion of the Southwest.* Albuquerque: University of New Mexico Press, 1973.

———. *Albuquerque.* Albuquerque: University of New Mexico Press, 1982.

———. *Following the Santa Fe Trail.* Santa Fe: Ancient City Press, 1984.

———, ed. *The Battle at Valle's Ranch: First Account of the Gettysburg of the West, 1862.* San Pedro Press, 1987.

Smith, Duane A. *The Birth of Colorado—A Civil War Perspective.* Norman: University of Oklahoma Press, 1989.

Stanley, F. *The Civil War in New Mexico.* Denver: The World Press, 1960.

Steinel, Alvin T. *A History of Agriculture in Colorado.* Fort Collins: State Agricultural College, 1926.

Stewart, James B. *Holy Warriors—Abolitionists and American Slavery.* New York: Hill and Wang, 1976.

Sumrall, Alan K. *Battleflags of Texans in the Confederacy.* Austin: Eakin Press, 1995.

Taylor, John M. *Bloody Valverde—A Civil War Battle on the Rio Grande.* Albuquerque: University of New Mexico Press, 1995.

Thomas, Dean S. *Cannons—An Introduction to Civil War Artillery.* Gettysburg: Thomas Publications, 1985.

Thompson, Jerry D. *Colonel John Robert Baylor: Texas Indian Fighter and Confederate Soldier.* Hillsboro: Hill Junior College, 1971.

———. *Henry Hopkins Sibley, Confederate General of the West.* Natchitoches: Northwestern State University Press, 1987.

———. *Desert Tiger: Captain Paddy Graydon and the Civil War in the Far Southwest.* El Paso: Texas Western Press, 1992.

Thrapp, Don L. *Encyclopedia of Frontier Biography.* Glendale, CA: Arthur H. Clark, 1988.

Twitchell, Ralph E. *Leading Facts of New Mexico History.* Vol. 2. Cedar Rapids: The Torch Press, 1912.

Wagner, Arthur L. *Organization and Tactics.* New York: Westerman, 1895.

Warner, Ezra J. *Generals in Grey.* Baton Rouge: Louisiana State University Press, 1959.

———. *Generals in Blue.* Baton Rouge: Louisiana State University Press, 1964.

Whitford, W. C. *Colorado Volunteers in the Civil War.* 1906; repr. Glorieta: Rio Grande Press, 1989.

Williams, Mrs. Ellen. *Three Years and a Half in the Army; or a History of the Second Colorados.* New York: Fowler and Wells, 1885.

Williams, Jerry L., ed. *New Mexico in Maps.* Albuquerque: University of New Mexico Press, 1986.

Woodhead, Henry, series director. *The Civil War.* 27 vols. Alexandria: Time-Life Books, 1985.

Wright, Arthur. *The Civil War in the Southwest.* Denver: Big Mountain Press, 1964.

Yeary, Mamie, ed. *Reminiscences of the Boys in Grey.* 1912; repr. Dayton: Morningside Press, 1986.

Articles

Alberts, Don E. "The Battle of Peralta." *New Mexico Historical Review* 58 (October 1983): 369–79.

Archambeau, Earnest R. Jr. "The New Mexico Campaign, 1861–1862." *Panhandle–Plains Historical Review* 37 (1964): 3–32.

Armstrong, Ruth. "Willard Andrews—for Love of New Mexico." *New Mexico Magazine* 60, no. 7 (July 1982): 40–45.

Bell, J. M. "The Campaign of New Mexico, 1862." In *War Papers Read Before the Commandery of the State of Wisconsin Military Order of the Loyal Legion of the United States,* 47–71. Milwaukee: Burdick, Armitage, and Allen, 1891.

Bloom, Lansing, ed. "Confederate Reminiscences." *New Mexico Historical Review* 5, no. 3 (July 1930): 315–24.

Boyd, Leroy. "Thunder on the Rio Grande, the Great Adventure of Sibley's Confederates for the Conquest of New Mexico and Colorado." *The Colorado Magazine* 24 (July 1947): 131–40.

Browne, P. D. "Captain T. D. Nettles and the Valverde Battery." *Texana* 2, no. 1 (Spring 1964): 1–23.

Charleton, Russell C. "The Civil War Years." *New Mexico Magazine* (April 1962): 32.

Chivington, John M. "The First Colorado Regiment." *New Mexico Historical Review* 33 (April 1958): 144–54.

Civil War Times Illustrated, ed. "The Pet Lambs at Glorieta Pass." *Civil War Times Illustrated* (November 1976): 30–37.

Donnell, F. S. "When Las Vegas was the Capital of New Mexico." *New Mexico Historical Review* 8, no. 4 (October 1933): 265–72.

Dorgan, Marion. "New Mexico's Fight for Statehood." *New Mexico Historical Review* 15, no. 2 (April 1940): 133–87.

Feynn, J. Robert. "A Soldier in New Mexico, 1860–1865." *El Palacio* 65 (August 1958): 143–45.

Hall, Martin H. "Colonel James Reily's Diplomatic Missions to Chihuahua and Sonora." *New Mexico Historical Review* 31, no. 3 (1956): 232–42.

———. "Notes and Documents—John M. Chivington." *New Mexico Historical Review* 33, no. 2 (April 1958): 144–55.

———. "Victory at Ft. Fillmore." *New Mexico Magazine* 39, no. 8 (August 1961): 20.

———. "Native American Relations in Confederate Arizona." *Journal of Arizona History* 8 (April 1967): 171–78.

———. "Negroes with Confederate Troops in West Texas and New Mexico." *Password* 13

(Spring 1968): 11–12.

———. "Planter vs. Frontiersman: Conflict in Confederate Indian Policy." In *Essays on the American Civil War,* ed. Frank E. Vandiver et al., 45–72. Austin: University of Texas Press, 1968.

———. "An Appraisal of the 1862 New Mexico Campaign: A Confederate Officer's Letter to Nacogdoches." *New Mexico Historical Review* 51, no. 4 (October 1976): 329–35.

Kajencki, Francis C. "Alexander Grzelachowski: Pioneer Merchant of Puerto de Luna, New Mexico." *Arizona and the West* 26 (Autumn 1984): 243–60.

———. "The Battle of Glorieta Pass: Was the Guide Ortiz or Grzelachowski?" *New Mexico Historical Review* 62, no. 1 (January 1987): 47–54.

Hayes, A. A. "The New Mexico Campaign of 1862, A Stirring Chapter of Our Late Civil War." *Magazine of American History* 15 (February 1886): 171–84.

Howard, James A. "New Mexico and Arizona Territories." *Journal of the West* 16 (April 1977): 85–100.

Hunsaker, William J. "Lansford W. Hastings' Project for the Invasion and Conquest of Arizona and New Mexico for the Southern Confederacy." *Arizona Historical Review* 4 (July 1931): 5–12.

Isern, Thomas D. "Colorado Territory." *Journal of the West* 16 (April 1977): 57–71.

James, H. L. "The Battle of Glorieta Pass, 1862." In *Archeology and History of Santa Fe County,* ed. Raymond V. Ingersoll. New Mexico Geological Society Special Publication no. 8 (1979): 17–18.

Jarrell, John. "Sibley and the Confederate Dream." *New Mexico Magazine* 54, no. 8 (August 1976): 18–22.

McLeary, J. H. "A History of Green's Brigade." Chapter 5 in *A Comprehensive History of Texas,* vol. 2., ed. Dudley G. Wooten. Dallas: William G. Scarff, 1898.

Miller, Darlis. "Hispanos and the Civil War in New Mexico—A Reconsideration." *New Mexico Historical Review* 54, no. 2 (1979): 105–23.

Morgan, James F. "The Lost Opportunity: The Confederate Invasion of New Mexico." *Confederate Veteran* (May–June 1987): 24–29.

Myers, Lee M. "New Mexico Volunteers: 1862–1866." *The Smoke Signal* 37 (1979). Tucson: Tucson Corral of the Westerners.

Oder, Broech N. "The New Mexico Campaign." *Civil War Times* (August 1978): 22–28.

Oliva, Leo E. "Chivington and the Mules at Johnson's Ranch." *Wagon Tracks—The Santa Fe Trail Association Quarterly* 6, (August 1992): 16–17.

Poldervaart, Arie. "Black-Robed Justice in New Mexico, 1846–1912." *New Mexico Historical Review* 22, no. 2 (April 1947): 109–39; and 22, no. 3 (July 1947): 286–314.

Porter, E. O. "Letters Home: W. W. Mills Writes to His Family." *Password* 17 (Spring 1972): 5–22; 17 (Summer 1972), 74–83; 17 (Fall 1972), 116–33; 17 (Winter 1972), 177–90.

Rogers, Robert L. "The Confederate States Organized in Arizona in 1862." *Southern Historical Society Papers* 28 (1900): 222–27.

Sanchez, Jane. "Agitated, Personal and Unsound." *New Mexico Historical Review* 41, no. 3 (July 1966): 217–30.

Santee, J. F. "The Battle of La Glorieta Pass." *New Mexico Historical Review* 6, no. 1 (January 1931): 66–75.

Starrett, J. S. "Letter to Robert Holman." *New Mexico Historical Review* (October 1957): 361–63.

Steere, Edward. "Rio Grande Campaign Logistics." *Military Review* (November 1953): 37–45.

Swanson, Betsy. "The Battles of Glorieta Pass." In *Pecos: Gateway to Pueblos and Plains, The Anthology,* eds. John V. Bezy and Joseph P. Sanchez. Tucson: Southwest Parks and Monuments Association, 1988.

Tate, Michael L., ed. "A Johnny Reb in Sibley's New Mexico Campaign: Reminiscences of

Private Henry C. Wright, 1861–1862." *East Texas Historical Review* 25 (1987): 20–33.

Thompson, Jerry. "The Vulture over the Carrion: Captain James 'Paddy' Graydon and the Civil War in the Territory of New Mexico." *Journal of Arizona History* 24 (Winter 1983): 381–401.

Waldrip, William I. "New Mexico During the Civil War." *New Mexico Historical Review* 28, no. 3 (July 1953): 163–291.

Walker, Charles. "Causes of the Confederate Invasion of New Mexico." *New Mexico Historical Review* 8, no. 2 (1967): 76–97.

Westphall, David. "The Battle of Glorieta Pass—Its Importance in the Civil War." *New Mexico Historical Review* 44, no. 2 (April 1969): 137–54.

"Why Did Colonel John P. Slough Resign?" *The Colorado Magazine* 39 (April 1962): 82–88.

Wilson, Spencer, and Robert A. Bieberman. "The Civil War in New Mexico: Tall Tales and True." In *Socorro Region II,* eds. Charles E. Chapin and Jonathan F. Callender. Thirty-fourth Field Conference, New Mexico Geological Society, Socorro New Mexico (1983), 85–87.

Wright, Arthur A. "Colonel John P. Slough and the New Mexico Campaign, 1862." *The Colorado Magazine* 39 (April 1962): 89–105.

Young, Bennett H. "Texas Cavalry Expedition in 1861–1862." *Confederate Veteran* 21 (March 1913): 16–19.

Miscellaneous

Andrews, Marshall. "Rates of Advance in Land Attack Against Unprepared Forces." Operations Research Office, Johns Hopkins University, 1960.

Colyer, Vincent. Line drawing entitled "Pigeon's Ranch—Famous Stopping Place enroute from Santa Fe to Fort Bascom, May 1869." Museum of Albuquerque accession number 85.30.5.

Edrington, Thomas S. "The Confederate Victory at Pigeon's Ranch." Brochure published by General William R. Scurry Camp—Sons of Confederate Veterans, March 28, 1987.

Giese, Dale F. "Echoes of the Bugle" A Bicentennial Booklet published by Phelps-Dodge Corporation. 1976; repr. 1991.

Helmbold, Robert L. "Rates of Advance in Historical Land Combat Operations." U.S. Army Concept Analysis Agency, Bethesda, MD. 1990.

The March of the First, Being a History of the Organization, Marches, Battles, and Service of the First Regiment of Colorado Volunteers by a Private of the Regiment. Denver: Thomas Gibson and Co., 1863.

Museum of New Mexico News Service. Attachment to undated news release on the reburial of Confederate soldiers entitled "Consolidated Forensic Data."

Owsley, Douglas W. "Bioarchaeology on a Battlefield: The Abortive Confederate Campaign in New Mexico." Museum of New Mexico, Office of Archaeological Studies, Archaeology Notes 142, 1994.

The Raguet Family—A private genealogical summary (courtesy Jerry Thompson).

Scott, Charles R. Unpublished letter to Mr. C. A. Dupree dated April 10, 1929 (courtesy S. A. Dupree).

Swanson, Betsy. "The Glorieta Battlefield." Unpublished manuscript of the Laboratory of Anthropology—Museum of New Mexico, 1986.

Wallen, Major Henry D. "1862 Ammunition Inventory of Fort Union" (courtesy Charles Meketa).

Index

Note: Individuals listed in the the casualty tables in the appendix are included in the index only if they have been referred to elsewhere in the text. Page numbers shown in italics indicate that the referenced item or person is on a map or figure.

Abo Pass, 109
Adair, Capt. Isaac, 103, 133, 135, *136*
Alamosa Creek, 111
Albuquerque, skirmish at, 109, 116
Albuquerque, *2*, 14, 16, 17, 19, *32*, *33*, 41, 109
  Confederate evacuation of, 110
  Confederate headquarters in, 34, 107, 108
  Confederate hospital in, 132
  Confederate occupation of, 24, 25, 31, 32, 34, 108, 132
  Federal evacuation of, 25, 26
Alexander, Capt. William, 133, *136*
Algodones, 132
Anthony, Capt. Scott, 44–*48*, *52*, 90, 124, *125*, 138
Anton Chico, *33*, 34
Apache Canyon, *2*, 34, 41–43, 50, 57, 92, 118
Apache Canyon, skirmish in, 41–55, 57, 60, 61
  burials, 51, 61, 68, 149n12
  casualties, 47, 49, 50, 51, 53, 57, 63, 68, 124, 125, 127, *128*, 132, 148n9, 148n20, 149n30, 155n21, 158n5, 159n15, 159n16
  Confederate order of battle, 126, *128*
  strategic bridge at, 51, *54*, 148n28
  truce following, 51, 59–61
  Union order of battle, 124, *125*
Aragon, Capt. Francisco, 25
Arizona, Territory of, *2*, 5, 8, 9, 11, 14, 17
Arizona Rangers, 41
Armijo, Manuel, 5, 92
artillery, 6, 9, 13, 28, 34, 36, 37, 60, 92, 114, 150n8, 152n36, 155n12, 157n28

Confederate at Apache Canyon, 43–*48*, 50, *52*, 55, 57, 126, *128*
Confederate at Johnson's Ranch, 92, 94, 140, 141, 155n20, 160n57
Confederate at Pigeon's Ranch, 68, 69, 72–*76*, 78, *79*, *81*, *85*, 133, 140
at Fort Craig and Valverde, 20–22
at skirmish at Albuquerque, 109, 110
Union at Pigeon's Ranch, 66, 70, 72, *74*, 75, 77–*79*, *81*–87, 129, 153n22, 159n17, 160n33
Bailey, Surg. Elisha, *129*
Baker, Lt. John, 73, 75, 130
Banks, Lt., 28
Barr, Lt. Samuel, 89, 138, *139*
Baylor, Col. John, 6–9, 11, 13, 14, 16, 17, 115
Beard Ranch, 57
Bennett, Lt. Jordan, 132, 148n14
Bent's Old Fort, 30
Bernal Springs, *33*, 36–38, 43, 60, 63, 104, 106, 150n3, 157n22
Bradford, Lt. James, 68, 69, *74*, 75, 103, 133, 134, *136*
Brigands, 41, 68, 118, 126, 133, *136*, 152n26
Brown, Pvt. George, 149n31
Buckholts, Capt. Charles, 73, 80, 103, 133, 134, *136*

California, *2*, 10, 11, 113
California Column, 116
Camp Lewis, 154n1
Camp Paul, 38
Camp Weld, *2*, 29, 30
Canadian River, *2*, *32*

Canby, Col. Edward, 15–17, 30
  actions following Glorieta, 108–110, 113, 114
  biographical information, 15, 145n9
  communication with Slough and Paul, 34, 36–38,
    87, 106, 157n22
  strategy for defense of New Mexico, 15–17, 19, 23,
    24, 30, 34
  at Valverde, 20–22
Canby, Louisa, 70, 105
Canoncito, 42, *119*
Carey, Capt. Asa, 89
Carleton, Col. James, 116, 146n8
Carleton, Sophia, 146n8
Carson, Col. Christopher "Kit", 16
Carson, Sgt. James, 80, 133, *136*, 153n8
Carnuel Pass, 109
casualties
  at Apache Canyon, 47, 49–51, 53, 63, 68, 124, 125,
    127, *128*, 132, 148n9, 148n20, 149n30, 155n21,
    158n5, 159n15, 159n16
  after Glorieta, 111
  at Johnson's Ranch, 94, 95, 97, 141, 155n20,
    155n21
  at Pigeon's Ranch, 73, 75, 76, 80, 84, 86, 87, 101–
    105, 118–*21*, 131, 137, 152n33, 153n19,
    159n25, 159n26
  at Valverde, 22, 50, 132, 145n21, 145n22
  prior to Valverde, 14
Cator, Pvt. Thomas, 68, 127
cavalry, 38, 39
  at Apache Canyon, 43–47, 50–*52*, 55
  at Glorieta, 64, 70–72, 77, 87, 150n6, 150n10,
    154n32
Cavillo, Pvt. Pancho, 140, 141, 160n56
Cerro de Escobas, 156n37
Chambers, Lt. Clark, 78, 84, 130, 153n19
Chapin, Capt. Gurden, 64, 70, 72, 86, 107, *129*,
    150n6, 152n24, 152n6
Chaves, Lt. Col. Manuel, 17, 28, 90, 92, 98, *99*, 124,
    125, 139, 147n8
Chihuahua, *2*, 10
Chivington, Maj. John, 38, *39*, 64
  at Apache Canyon, 43–45, 47, *48*, 50, 51, 55, 57,
    60–62, 124, *125*
  biographical information, 38, 116, 117
  expectation of arrival at Battle of Pigeon's Ranch,
    78, 96, 97, 153n13
  at Johnson's Ranch, 92–94, 97, 138, *139*, 155n16,

    155n18, 155n24, 155n27
  march to and from Johnson's Ranch, 70, 89, 90,
    92, *93*, 95–100, 154n32, 155n12, 156n32
  promotion of, 107
Claflin, Capt. Ira, 66, 72, *74*, 75, 77–*79*, *81*, 82, 84–
    86, 129, 152n6
Cobb, Lt. Alfred, 97, 98, *129*, 156n34, 156n36
Collins, Col. James, 90, 109, *125, 139*, 155n27
Colorado, Territory of, *2*, 10, 17, 28, 29, *32*
Colorado Volunteers (*see also* First Regiment, Colo-
    rado Volunteers and Second Regiment, Colo-
    rado Volunteers), 16, 21, 28–30, *71*, 115–17
Confederate Army of New Mexico (*see also* Sibley
    Brigade), 13, 14, *33*, 41, 90, 109, 110
Connelly, Gov. Henry, 15, 24, 28, 31, 110
Cook, Capt. Samuel, 39, 42, 44, *46–48*, 50, 51, *71*, 77,
    124, *125*
Coopwood, Capt. Bethel, 34
Crosson, Capt. James, 133, *136*
Cubero, 25, 26, 34, 108, 132

Davidson, Pvt. William, 11, *27*, 60, 68, 95, 105, 115,
    132, 135
  at Apache Canyon, 43, 50, 51
  biographical information, 25, 118
  describes Battle of Pigeon's Ranch, 70, 71, 73
Davis, Pres. Jefferson, 9, 103
DeForrest, Lt. Cyrus, 90
Denver City, *2*, 29, 31, *32*
Dickinson, Lt. Eli, 75
Dodd, Capt. Theodore, 21, 30
Donaldson, Maj. James, 24, 26, 28, 30, 145n4
Downing, Capt. Jacob, 49, 158n12
  at Apache Canyon, 44, *46–48*, *52*, 55, 57, 124, *125*
  biographical information, 44, 117
  at Pigeon's Ranch, 72, *74*, 75, 77, *79*, *81*–87, 101,
    129, 152n28, 153n7
Dry Creek, *2*, 30, *32*
Duncan, Maj. Thomas, 21

El Paso, *2*, 6, 14, 144n4, 158n12
Enos, Capt. Herbert,
  at Pigeon's Ranch, 64, 66, 70, 72, 84, 129, 150n3,
    153n22
  evacuates Albuquerque, 25, 26
Falvey, Lt. John, 90, 138, *139*, 154n32, 154n4,
    155n11
Farmer, Pvt. J. E., 87

Fifth Regiment, New Mexico Volunteers, 17
Fifth Regiment, Texas Mounted Volunteers, 13, 21,
    23, 25, 34, 45, 55, 57, 68, 108
    Company A, 41, 43, 47–51, 80, 95, 126, *128*, 133,
        136, 148n14, 153n8
    Company B, 21, 41, 126, *128*, 133, *136*
    Company C, 41, 47, 126, *128*, 133, *136*
    Company D, 41, 126, *128*, 133, *136*
    Company I, 94
Fifth United States Infantry, 15, 16
    Company A, 89, 138, *139*, 160n33
    Company E, 160n33
    Company G, 89, 138, *139*, 160n33
First Regiment, Colorado Volunteers, 29–32, 35, 37,
    57, 61, 107, 146n25, 149n31
    Company A, 29, 39, 44, 47, 90, 97, 124, *125*, 138,
        139
    Company B, 30, 89, 138, *139*
    Company C, 72, 77, 78, 83, 97, *129*
    Company D, 39, 44, 47, 72, 75–78, 83, 87, 124,
        125, *129*, 152n28, 153n7
    Company E, 39, 44, 47, 90, 124, *125*, 138, *139*,
        159n26
    Company F, 39, 42–44, 47, 50, 51, 53–55, 77, 83,
        87, 124, *125*, *129*, 159n17
    Company G, 77, 78, 83, *129*
    Company H, 90, 94, 138, *139*
    Company I, 72, 73, 76, *129*, 152n33
    Company K, 72, 77, *129*
First Regiment, New Mexico Volunteers, 16
First United States Cavalry, 16, 47, 87, 124, *125*, 129,
    150n10
flags, Confederate, 29, 43, 120, *121*, 148n10
Foard, Capt. William, 133, *136*
Ford, Capt. James, 28, 30, *71*, 90, 138, *139*, 154n5
Ford, Col. John, 6
Forked Lightning Ranch (*see* Kozlowski's Ranch)
Fort Bliss, 6, 14
Fort Breckenridge, 6
Fort Buchanan, 6
Fort Clark, 6
Fort Conrad, 20, 145n17
Fort Craig, *2*, 111, 114, 157n22
    Confederate objective, 9, 14, 15, 17, 23, 109
    garrison at, 16
    history and description, 14
    involvement in Battle of Valverde, 20, 22, 23, 30
Fort Davis, 6

Fort Fauntleroy, 6
Fort Fillmore, *2*, 6, 7
Fort Lancaster, 6
Fort Leavenworth, 15
Fort McLane, 6, 7
Fort Marcy, 145n14
Fort Stanton, *2*, 7, 109
Fort Stockton, 6
Fort Thorn, *2*, 20
Fort Union, *2*, 9, 26, 115
    arrival of Coloradans, 28, 31, 35
    Confederate advance on, 32–34
    Confederate objective, 17, 60, 109, 113–15
    debate on defense of, 36–38, 104, 106, 114
    garrison of, 16, 19
    history and description, 17–19, 145n14
    star fort, 17, *18*, 28, 114
    Union sortie from, 37
Fort Wise, *2*, 30, *32*
Fourth Regiment, New Mexico Volunteers, 17, 19,
    66, 89, 90, 150n10
    Company G, 138, *139*, 154n5
Fourth Regiment, Texas Mounted Volunteers, 13, 21,
    23, 34, 57, 58, 68, 69, 73, 89, 90, 110, *136*
    Company A, 34
    Company B, 133
    Company C, 69, 73, 133
    Company D, 71, 133
    Company E, 73, 80, 133
    Company F, 58, 95, 102, 133
    Company G, 133, 140
    Company H, 133
    Company I, 133
    Company K, 133
Fulcrod, Lt. Phil, 58

Galisteo Creek, 42, 60, 92, 149n9
Galisteo road, 60, 64, 90, *93*, 97, 98
Galisteo, *33*, 34, 57, 60, 90, 95, 149n2, 155n11
Gardiner, Pvt. Charles, 97
Gardner, Capt. James, 133, *136*
Garson, Greer, 118
Gettysburg, analogy to, 4, 78, 113, 114, 122, 143n1
Giesecke, Capt. Julius, 133, 136
Gilpin, Gov. William, 29, 39
Glorieta Baptist Center, *119*
Glorieta Creek, 90
Glorieta Mesa, 41, 59, 64, 89, 90, 92–94, 97, 98,

154n10, 155n12, 155n17, 156n37
Glorieta Pass, *2*, *33*, 41, 61, 62, 68, 69, 118
Glorieta Pass, Battle of, 22, 116
    burial of dead, 51, 61, 68, 102, 149n12
    casualties at Apache Canyon, 47, 49–51, 53, 63,
        68, 124, 125, 148n9, 148n20, 149n30, 155n21,
        158n5, 159n15, 159n16
    casualties at Johnson's Ranch, 94, 95, 97, 141,
        155n20, 155n21
    casualties at Pigeon's Ranch, 73, 75, 76, 80, 84,
        101–105, 118–*21*, 131, 137, 152n33, 153n19,
        159n25, 159n26
    compared to Gettysburg, 4, 78, 113, 114, 122,
        143n1
    roadside marker, 113
    significance of, 4, 113, 114, 122
Glorieta, 42, *119*
Green, Col. Tom, *20*, 25, *33*, 34, 90, 93, 108, 110
    biographical information, 13
    at Valverde, 21, 22
Grzelachowski, Alexander, 98–*100*, 109, 156n36,
    156n37, 156n38

Hamilton, Dr. John, *71*
Hampton, Capt. George, 133, *136*
Hanna, Pvt. Ebenezer, 25, 134
Hardeman, Lt. Col. William, 34, 110
Hardin, Lt. George, 78
Hoffmann, Capt. Gustave, 68, *79*, *85*, 132, 133, *136*,
    149n2
Holcomb, Pvt. Harvey, 58, 95, 101, 105
Holland, Lt. James, 133, *136*
Hollister, Pvt. Ovando, 44, 75, 87, 89, 106, 155n11
Howland, Capt. George, 24, 39
    at Apache Canyon, 44–*48*, *52*, 55, 124, *125*
    at Pigeon's Ranch, 64, 70, 129, 150n6, 152n24
Hume, Pvt. William, 43, *128*, 148n14
Hunter, Maj. Gen. David, 30
Hunter, Maj. Sherod, 118

Indian Pacification Commission, 117
Indians, problems with, 6, 8, 9, 14, 17, 116, 117

Jackson, Maj. Alexander, 101, 156n2
Jett, Lt. William, 126, 151n14
Johnson, Pres. Andrew, 116
Johnson, Anthony, 42, 63
Johnson's Ranch, *2*, 42, 47, 51, 57, 59, 63, 64, 118

Texan camp at, 55, 60, 66, 92, 151n13
Johnson's Ranch, raid on, 89–100, 154n10, 155n16
    casualties at, 94, 95, 97, 141, 155n20, 155n21
    Confederate hospital at, 66, 95, 140, 155n21
    Confederate order of battle, 140, 141
    destruction of wagons and slaughter of mules at,
        96, 97, 155n27
    Union march to and, from, 70, 89, 90, 92, *93*, 95–
        100, 154n32, 155n12, 156n32, 156n34, 156n37
    Union order of battle, 138, *139*
    Union plan for, 64, 92, 93, 150n4
Jones, Rev. Lucius, 95, 140, 141
Jordan, Maj. Powhatan, 34, 132, 149n2
Jornado del Muerto, *2*, 14
Josephy, Alvin (describes Brigands), 41

Kansas, Military Department of, 30
Kansas, State of, 28
Kansas, Territory of, *2*, 17, 28
Kavenaugh, Dr. F. E., 25
Kearney, Gen. Stephen, 11, 92
Kelly, Pvt., 75
Kerber, Lt. Charles, 72–*74*, *129*
Kirk, Pvt. Thomas, 71
Kirk, Pvt. William, 78, 134
Kozlowski, Napoleon, 39, 63, 104, 147n44
Kozlowski's Ranch, *2*, 42, *93*, 118, *119*
    Chivington's return to, 98–100, 104, 156n36,
        156n37
    field hospital at, 104
    Slough's return to, 86
    Union camp at, 62, 63, 100–102, 104
    Union march to, 39, 150n3
    Union movement from, 64, 66, 70, 89

Lamar, 30
lancers at Valverde, 21, 30
La Glorieta Pass (*see* Glorieta Pass)
Lane, Lt. Ellsberry, 134, *136*
Lang, Capt. Willis, 21
Las Vegas, *2*, 28, *32*, *33*, 37, 38, 98
Lemitar, 24
Leseur, Capt. Charles, 133, *136*
Lewis, Capt. William, 36, 64
    evacuates Santa Fe, 28
    at Johnson's Ranch, 89, 94, 97, 138, *139*, 155n16,
        155n18, 155n20, 155n24, 155n27
    movement to Glorieta Pass, 37, 61

Little, Sgt. George, 51
Lockridge, Maj. Samuel, 22
Logan, Capt. Samuel, 89, *91*, 138, *139*
logistics, 6, 15, 17
 Confederate between Valverde and Glorieta, 22–
  26, 28, 34, 61, 66, 147n4, 151n13
 Confederate after Glorieta, 105, 106, 108, 109,
  114–16, 122
 Union, 14, 24, 61, 66, 70, 84, 86, 153n22
Loma, 37
Lord, Capt. Richard, 24, 47, *48, 52*, 66, 87, 124, *125*,
 150n10, 154n31
Loring, Gen. William, 15, 144n8
Los Lunas, village of, 25, 26, 110
Los Pinos, village of, 110
Lynde, Maj. Isaac, 7, *8*

McGrath, Lt. Peter, 75
McGuiness, Sgt. Joseph, 132, 148n14
McIntyre, Lt. John, 42, 43, 148n9
McKee, Surg. James, 7
McKinney, Pvt. James, 68, 127
McLeary, Pvt. James, 50, 127, 132, 159n12
McNeill, Lt. Col. Henry, 23, 24
McRae, Capt. Alexander, 21
McRae's Battery, 21, *22*
Mailie, Capt. Charles, 72
Manzano, village of, 98, 109, 110
Marshall, Lt. William, 50, 124
Mesilla, *2*, 5, 14, 41, 109, 111, 115, 144n4
Mesilla, skirmish at, 7
Mesilla Times, 8
Mexican-American War, 4, 9, 13, 15, 35, 90, 92
Miller, Sgt. John, 51
Monterey, Battle of, 13, 145n4
Mormons, campaign against, 9, 15

Nelson, Lt. George, 39, 42, 43, 50, 57, 77–*79, 81*, 84,
 85, 129
Nettles, Pvt. Timothy
 at Apache Canyon, 43, *52*, 148n14
 at Johnson's Ranch, 94, 126, *128*, 141, 155n20,
  160n57
New Mexico
 Military Department of, 10, 15–17, 28, 66
 Territory of, *2*, 15, 103
  pre-war attitudes, 4, 5
  Confederate invasion strategy, 14

  Territorial Legislature, 155n27
  Union defense of, 6, 20
New Mexico Militia, 16, 24, 26, 28
New Mexico Volunteers (*see* also specific units), 15–
 17, 20, 26, 28, 124
Nicodemus, Capt. William, 157n22
Norman, Pvt. Adolphus, 43, 44, 50, *128*, 148n14
Norvell, Lt. Stephen, 89, 138, *139*

Oakes, Lt. Pleasant, 132, 153n8
Ochiltree, Lt. Thomas, 103, 104, 115
Odell, Capt. James, 133, 134
Oklahoma Territory, 17
Oliva, Leo, 97
Overton Sharp-Shooter, 114, 115, 118
Owings, Dr. Lewis, 5

Padre Springs Creek, 156n37
Paraje, 20
Patrick, Sgt. John, 78
Paul, Col. Gabriel, 16, 28, 31, 110
 biographical information, 35, 147n35
 interactions with Slough, 34–37, 106, 107
Pecos Church, 39
Pecos Pueblo, 90, *119*
Pecos River, *2*, 24, 34, 39
Pecos, 42
Pelham, William, 28, 146n13
Peralta, skirmish at, 110, 116, 118
Peticolas, Sgt. Alfred, 69, 72, 80, 82, 111, 118, 120,
 153n13,, 153n14
Phillips, Capt. John, 41, 118, 126, 133, *136*
Pierce, Pvt. George, 80
Pigeon, the (*see* Valle, Alexander)
Pigeon's Ranch (*see* also Valle's Ranch), 2, 59, *93*,
 119, 157n32
 description of, 42, 60, 63, *65*, 118, 151n22
 Union arrival at, 60, 61, 70
 use as field hospital, 60, 61, 63, 70
Pigeon's Ranch, Battle of, 63–87, 102, 116, 155n11
 burials at, 102, 118–*21*
 casualties at, 73, 75, 76, 80, 84, 101–105, 118–*21*,
  131, 137, 152n33, 153n19, 159n25, 159n26
 Confederate order of battle, 132, 133
 expectation of Chivington's participation in, 96,
  97
 importance of, 113–16
 phase 1, 71–76

phase 2, 77–84
phase 3, 84–87, 153n22
truce following 101, 102, 105
Union order of battle, *129*
Pino, Col. Miguel, 16
Pino, Col. Nicholas, 24
police guard, 78, *129*, 150n10, 154n5
Polvadera, supply depot at, 24
Purgatoire River, 31
Pyron's bastion, 47, *53*, 55, 75
Pyron, Maj. Charles, *35*, 89
    advance to Glorieta Pass, *33*, 34, 41, 42
    at Apache Canyon, 43–49, 51, *52*, 55, 57, 58, 60,
      126, *128*, 147n8
    biographical information, 14, 117
    at Pigeon's Ranch, *68, 69, 74*, 75, 78, *79, 81, 85*,
      103, 133, *136*, 156n2
    at Valverde, 21

Ragsdale, Capt. Dan, 126, *128*, 133, *136*
Raguet, Maj. Henry, *69*
    actions at Pigeon's Ranch, 68, 69, *74*, 78, *79, 81–*
      83, 85, 86, 133, *136*, 151n20
    actions at Valverde, 21
    death of, 86, 87, 103, 134
Rancho de la Glorieta (*see* Pigeon's Ranch)
Raton Pass, *2*, 31, *32*
Reeve, Lt. Col. I. V. D., 6
Regiment of Mounted Rifles, 7, 15
Reily, Col. James, 13
Rencher, Gov. Abraham, 4
Rio Abajo Press, 155n27
Rio Grande, *2*, 6, 9, 14, 17, 20, 21, *33*, 34, 109–111
Rio Puerco, 110
Ritter, Capt. John, 66, 72, *74*, 75, 77–79, *81*–86, 129,
    152n6
Ritter, Pvt. Simon, 97, 138
Robbins, Capt. Samuel, *71*, 72, *74*, 75, 77, *79, 81*, 84,
    85, 129
Roberts, Lt. Col. Benjamin, *20*, 21
Rynerson, Col. William, 116

San Antonio, Texas, 6, 9, 10, 14, 115, 117, 118
San Antonio, New Mexico, *33*, 36
San Augustin Pass, *2*, 7, 16
San Cristobal Canyon, 90, 154n10
San Elizario Spy Company, 34
San Jose, 39

Sanborn, Capt. George, 90, 138
Sand Creek Massacre, 95, 116, 117
Sandia, Pueblo of, 26
Sanford, Lt. Byron, 90, 94, 155n20
Sangre de Cristo Mountains, *2*, 41
San Mateo Mountains, *2*, 111
Santa Cruz Valley, Arizona, 8
Santa Fe, *2*, 14, 17, 19, 25, *32, 33*, 93, 94, 104, 116,
    117, 145n14
    evacuated by Confederate forces, 110
    evacuated by Union forces, 24, 26, 28, 30
    hospital at, 105, 108, 132
    occupation by Confederates, 31, 38, 41, 70, 71,
      108, 109, 151n14
    return to by Confederate forces, 105
Santa Fe Gamblers (*see* Brigands)
Santa Fe Gazette, 5, 105, 106, 115, 155n20, 155n27
Santa Fe National Cemetery, 119–*21*
Santa Fe Railroad, 118, *119*
Santa Fe Trail, *2*, 17, *32*, 34, 39, 41, 42, *46*, 63, 64, 69,
    89, 90, *93*, 94, 101, 104, 118, 145n14
Sapp, Pvt. Perry, 47, 159n15
Schwarzhoff, Lt. Scipio, 133, *136*
Scott, Lt. John, 126, *127*, 133, *136*
Scurry, Col. William, *59*, 92, 93, 96
    actions following Battle of Pigeon's Ranch, 103,
      105, 108, 114
    advance to Glorieta Pass, 33, 34, 51, 57–61, 89
    at Battle of Pigeon's Ranch, 66, 68–70, 73, *74*, 76–
      83, *85*, 101, 102, 132, 133, *136*, 151n20, 156n2
    at Battle of Valverde, 21, 23
    biographical information, 13, 117
    reaction to raid on Johnson's Ranch, 95, 102
Second Regiment, Colorado Volunteer Infantry, 30
Second Regiment, New Mexico Volunteers, 16, 17,
    28, 90, 98, 147n8
Second Regiment, Texas Mounted Volunteers, 6, 14,
    21, 57, 151n14
    Company B, 14, 41, 126, 140
    Company D, 34
    Company E, 41, 126, 140
Seventh Regiment, Texas Mounted Volunteers, 13,
    14, 34, 58, 68, 69, 73, 144n4, 149n2
    Company A, 14, 26, 34
    Company B, 14, 80, 133, 140, 160n56
    Company F, 14, 133
    Company H, 14, 133
    Company I, 14, 66, 133

Seventh United States Infantry, 7, 15, 16, 70

Shaffer, Lt. James, *71*, 90, 138

Shannon, Capt. Denman, 47, 80, *82*, 103, 126, *128*, 133, 135, *136*, 153n11, 157n8

Sharpshooters' Ridge, 77, 78, 83, 84, 86, 87, 119

Shropshire, Maj. John, *35*
   advances to Glorieta Pass, 34, 41, 42
   at Apache Canyon, 43–45, 48–50, *52*, 55, 57, 126, *128*
   biographical information, 34, 49, 153n8
   death and burial of, 80, 103, 120, 135
   at Pigeon's Ranch, 68, *74*, 78–82, 133, *136*

Sibley Brigade (*see also* Confederate Army of New Mexico), 11, 13, 14, 111, 117, 118

Sibley, Brig. Gen. Henry Hopkins, *10*, 93
   biographical information, 9, 15, 117, 145n9
   blamed for failure of campaign, 114–16
   campaign objectives and strategy, 9–11, 13–15, 17, 20, 22, 23, 32, 90, 108, 113
   concern for logistics, 22, 26, 28, 32
   plan for attacking Fort Union, 32–34, 41, 109
   retreat from New Mexico, 109–111, 113
   at Valverde, 20, 21

Slough, Col. John, *37*, 43, 156n34
   advances to Glorieta Pass, 37, 38, 60–64
   biographical information, 29, 30, 116
   command at Pigeon's Ranch, *129*
   interactions with Canby and Paul, 35–38, 87, 157n22
   march to Fort Union, 30–32
   at Pigeon's Ranch, 64, 70, 72, 76, 77, *79*, 84–87, 96, 97, 101, 107, *129*, 150n3, 153n22
   resignation of, 106, 107
   retreat from Pigeon's Ranch, 104, 106, 114
   strategy for engaging Scurry, 64, 77, 78, 87, 89, 96

Smiley, Jerome C., 143n1

Smith, Pvt. William, 107, 108

Socorro, Confederate hospital at, 132

Socorro, skirmish at, 24

Socorro, 23, 24

Sonora, 10, 13

Sopris, Capt. Richard, 72, *74*, 77, *79, 81, 85*, 129

Soule, Capt. Silas, *71*

Southworth, Surg. Malek, *136*

Stafford, Capt. Isaac, 126, 151n14

Starr, Pvt. Frank, 86

Steele, Col. William, 144n4

Stivers, Capt. Charles, 153n11

strategic bridge (at Apache Canyon), 51, *54*, 148n28

Sullock, Pvt. John, 128, 159n14

Sumner, Lt. Col. Edwin, 17

supplies (*see* logistics)

Sutton, Lt. Col. John, 14, 22

Taos Rebellion, 90

Tappan, Lt. Col. Samuel, *67*
   activities after Glorieta, 107
   biographical information, 30, 64, 66, 117, 146n22
   at Pigeon's Ranch, 64, 70, 72, *74*, 78–82, 84, 96, 120, 129, 153n13, 153n20, 159n17,

Taylor, Lt. John, 66, 94, 140, 141, 151n13

Teel, Maj. Trevanion, 10, 11, 68, 113, 115

Tenth United States Infantry, 16

Terrell, Pvt. Samuel, 49, 68, 128, 159n12

Texan-Santa Fe Expedition, 5, 14

Texas, Confederate State of, *2*, 17
   recruitment of troops in, 6, 9, 13
   withdrawal of Federal forces from, 6

Third Regiment, New Mexico Volunteers, 17

Third United States Cavalry, 16, 44, 47, 57, 87, 124, *125*, 129
   Company E, 28, 124
   Company K, 89, 90, 138, *139*

Thurmond, Capt. Alfred, 25, 26, 34

Tijeras Canyon, 110

Tijeras, *33*

Tinkler, Pvt. J. W. "Wat", 127, 159n12

Tooke, Sgt. Lovard, 50, 127, 159n12

Trinidad, 31

Tucson, 5, 8

Tyler, Pvt. B. H., 102

Valle, Alexander, 42, 63, 118

Valle's Ranch (*see* Pigeon's Ranch)

Valverde Battery, 148n14

Valverde, Battle of, 21–23, 30, 66, 84, 86, 90, 116
   casualties, 22, 23, 50, 132, 145n21, 145n22
   implications for Battle of Glorieta, 22, 114, 115

Valverde ford, 20, 145n17

Van Dorn, Gen. Earl, 9, 10

Walker, Capt. Charles, 66
   at Apache Canyon, 44, *46*, *48*, *52*, 124, *125*
   before Glorieta, 28, 36
   at Pigeon's Ranch, 64, 70, 72, 87, 150n6, 150n10, 154n29

Walker, Capt. James, 34
Walker, Pvt. "Doc", 50, 127
Walsenburg, 30
Wells, Capt. Stephen, *48*, 49, 126–*28*, 153n8
White, Pvt. Benjamin, 73, 134
Whitford, William, 61, 86, 87, 119, 120, 140
Wiggins, Capt. J. F., 133, *136*

Wilder, Capt. William, 77, 78, 84, *85*
Wright, Pvt. H. C., 97
Wright, Lt. Thomas, 132, 153n8
Wynkoop, Capt. Edward, *45, 71*
    at Apache Canyon, 44, *46–48, 52*, 124, *125*
    biographical information, 44, 117
    at Johnson's Ranch, 90, 94, 138, *139*